WEIRD STORIES FROM REAL LIFE

Marjorie Burns, ed.

SCHOLASTIC INC.
New York Toronto London Auckland Sydney

For reprint permission, grateful acknowledgment is made to:

Garrett Publications and the Estate of Nandor Fodor for the excerpt from THE HAUNTED MIND by Nandor Fodor, copyright by Garrett Publications, New York.

Harper & Row, Publishers, Inc. for the abridged adaptation from pp. 90-93 of KINSHIP WITH ALL LIFE by J. Allen Boone, copyright, 1954 by Harper & Row, Publishers, Inc.

ISBN 0-590-10429-2

12 11 10   0 1/9

CONTENTS

INTRODUCTION

"All of us have mildly weird experiences, but most of us don't know it." So says a scientist who has made a study of such "mildly weird" experiences as:

Telepathy — direct mind-to-mind communication without the use of language (we usually think it's just coincidence).

Clairvoyance — "clearly seeing" something that is out of physical eyeshot (we usually call it imagination).

Precognition — knowing what is going to happen before it happens (we usually explain it away as a hunch or a lucky guess).

In this book you'll read stories about people who had these mildly weird experiences. But you'll also read about people who had such violently weird experiences as:

Telekinesis — the movement of objects without physical contact, often called "mind over matter." Sometimes, as in poltergeist cases, the telekinetic power seems to come from somebody's subconscious mind.

Ghosts and apparitions — by definition, a ghost is the surviving spirit of a dead person, while an apparition is just an "appearance," or vision. People who have seen either one say that it's hard to tell which is which.

Astral projection — the separation of the mind from the physical body. People who have experienced this claim that the mind puts on an astral body (which may be something like an electromagnetic field) and goes traveling, leaving the physical body home in bed.

Unless you belong to a very small minority of the human race, you have never had a violently weird experience. Reading these stories should make you glad you haven't.

DO YOU HAVE ESP?

by Margaret Ronan

You walk to the telephone to call a friend. But before you can take the receiver off the hook, the phone rings. It's the same friend, calling you.

At the last minute, you give in to a "hunch" and cancel out on a music festival date. The car in which you planned to travel gets involved in an accident on the way.

You dream you are sitting in class watching the teacher write three questions on the board. The next day those same questions turn up in a surprise test.

Have experiences like these ever happened to you? Every one of them has happened to teenagers I know. And other teenagers have told me of even weirder happenings, such as going to a strange town and knowing, without being told, where certain streets and buildings are, or getting advance notice, in a dream, of a relative's death.

Some people lump all these happenings together under the label of *coincidence*. Others say such "coincidences" are really cases of ESP (Extra-Sensory Perception). If you have ESP, you can sometimes seem to pick up information without any help from your five senses — touch, taste, sight, hearing, and smell. You may have an uncanny knack for guessing right answers, or picking winners. You may somehow "know" what people are thinking, or what they're going to say even before they say it. Perhaps once in a while you have a dream that comes true.

There is more than one kind of ESP. There's *telepathy*, a kind of mind-to-mind communication without spoken or written words. There's *precognition*, or foreseeing future events. There's *clairvoyance*, or sensing people, places, or things which actually exist but which are hidden from you or too far away for you to know about. There's *psychometry*, or holding an object in your hand and "reading" its history — who owned it, what happened to that person, etc. And there's *psychokinesis*, a kind of mind-over-matter power that makes it possible to move objects by will power alone.

Is ESP for real? For years scientists at the Institute for Parapsychology have been trying to answer that question. In 1930, at Duke University in Durham, North Carolina, they began ESP experiments to prove there was no such thing. But according to Dr. J. B. Rhine, the Institute's director, 40 percent of those early tests seemed to show that there was such a thing as "psychic" ability.

ESP isn't easy to investigate. Even those who have it can't always turn it on when they want to.

Because they can't put ESP under a microscope, scientists have had to come up with other ways of measuring ESP ability. One such method uses the Zener cards, named after Dr. K. E. Zener, a colleague of Dr. Rhine's. There are 25 cards in a Zener deck, marked with five different symbols (each symbol appears on five cards): a circle, a rectangle, a plus sign, three horizontal wavy lines, and a star.

In most Zener card experiments, one volunteer acts as a "sender" and the other as a "receiver." The sender sits in one room, draws a card, and makes a note of the symbol on it. He tries to "send" a mental picture of the symbol to the receiver. The receiver concentrates and makes a note of the symbol that comes into his mind.

It's easy to test your own ESP. You don't even need a deck of Zener cards — you can use ordinary playing cards. What you can't get along without, however, is a cooperative friend who will act as the sender.

To test yourself, choose 20 cards. If you're using ordinary playing cards, take five of each suit. Give them to your friend and ask him or her to go into the next room. Have the sender shuffle and cut the cards, then lay them face down on a table. He should then pick up the top card, say, "Ready," loudly enough so you can hear, and concentrate on the picture on the card.

On a sheet of paper, record what you think the picture is. If, for example, it is the five of hearts, write down "5" and "H." (The sender should also keep a written record of each card he draws.) Then call out, "Next," so the sender can draw and concentrate on the next card.

After you have recorded your guesses on all 20 cards, compare your record with the one kept by the sender. Scientists say one right guess out of five can be due to chance. But if you score above 20 percent, something more than chance could be at work. And if 40 to 50 percent of your guesses are right, that "something" could be ESP!

HOW I READ THE TAROT

by Juliette Callefille

Just before I sat down to write this article, I took out my favorite deck of Tarot cards and did a reading. Choosing a card with a woman's face to represent myself, I placed it in the middle of the table. Then I shuffled the remaining cards, concentrating on a question — as it happened, a question about money. I cut the cards into three piles, then combined them into one again, all with my left hand. Why the left? I don't know, but it's been done that way by Tarot readers for thousands of years, so I followed tradition. From the top of the deck I took the first ten cards and spread them in a pattern said to have originated centuries ago with the Celts, a people who domi-

5

nated Europe from about the 5th to the 1st century B.C. Then I studied the cards.

I have spent years learning the traditional meanings of the Tarot cards, but I also allowed my own mind and emotions to respond to what I saw before me. The message was that I would soon have an opportunity to start a new, creative enterprise that might bring me money, and that the chance would come through a woman. However, there was some opposition possible, from a man.

I put the cards aside and started to type. There was a knock at my office door, and I turned to see an editor I know. She had come to offer me a writing job. But there was a catch: I would get the job only if a man, who had previously contracted to do it, failed to come back from a long journey in time to meet his obligation!

I've been interested in the Tarot — a deck of 78 cards bearing ancient symbols — ever since I saw the old movie *Nightmare Alley*, in which Joan Blondell read Tyrone Power's fortune. As I recall, Miss Blondell called the cards the Tar*it*. When correctly pronounced, the word rhymes with "narrow"; however, the accent may be on either the first or last syllable. She also seemed to consider the Hanged Man the worst card in the deck, which it isn't. It stands for sacrifice, but not necessarily for disaster.

6

Years later I read some of the works of the great psychiatrist Carl Jung; T. S. Eliot's famous poem "The Waste Land"; and a novel by Charles Williams called *The Greater Trumps*. All referred to the Tarot, and my appetite was whetted.

Eventually I got hold of a deck of Tarot cards and began to learn the meanings that people have seen in their symbols for, it's thought, as long as 3,500 years. Just to try them out, one day, I agreed to do a reading for a girl who worked near me, whom I knew only slightly. All the cards pointed to loss and disappointment, urged care with material possessions, indicated that someone was putting her at some kind of disadvantage. She went home about an hour later and found that her apartment had been robbed!

A few weeks ago I attended a lecture, given by a highly respected psychiatrist, on the current interest in mysticism and the occult. At the end the speaker asked if anyone in the room had had any experience with such matters. I had done a reading for a friend just before the talk, and had my Tarot cards with me. When I admitted it, someone in the audience of about 200 people called out, "Give us a demonstration."

A woman sitting near a table volunteered to be the "guinea pig," and I gave her the cards to shuffle. But first I explained that in such a confusing atmosphere, where concentration was very difficult, and with only a few seconds to study the cards, I couldn't give much of a reading. I would just spread the cards to show how a reading worked.

I spread them in the simplest way possible — seven cards in a straight line — turned them over, and read that the woman was involved in some kind of creative work that would bring her money, but that she might spoil it by being too greedy. I also read that, in the past, she had made a decision to renounce some deeply held belief that had meant a great deal to her, and that the decision had profoundly affected her life. I was just starting to say again, "This is only an idea of what a reading might be like —" when the woman, looking shocked, said, "It's true! It's all true."

What makes such things happen? How does the Tarot work? Many people think that the cards have some mystical power that comes alive in the hands of the person who touches them. But there is a more scientific explanation — if, with many serious scientists all over the world, you concede that there may be "something to" ESP.

Personally, I think it's possible that two forms of ESP operate in a Tarot reading. Let's take the case of Jeanne, the girl whose apartment was robbed. Without realizing it, Jeanne was probably getting very strong telepathic messages from the mind of the thief who was stealing from her. He was in the midst of objects she cared about, and had often touched. He was in an atmosphere very familiar to her. He was willing her not to come home, and planning what he would do if she did come in and surprise him. Jeanne may even have picked up a message from his mind when he began to think about robbing her apartment, before he actually entered it. And I, the reader, sitting beside her, deliberately emptying my own mind so that I might tune in on her thoughts, picked up the messages, too. That's where telepathy may have come in.

When Jeanne touched the Tarot cards, something related to clairvoyance may have come into play. She had never even looked at Tarot cards before — but her fingers found the right ones, the ones that would tell me what was in her mind, what she was picking up from her environment, or what was stored in her own subconscious. If, as some students of the occult believe, the Tarot symbols are universal and form a part of the subconscious of every human being, Jeanne may have "known" which symbols expressed the forces that were in play around her.

Or, it could be that I, who *have* studied the symbols, helped her — all without words — to choose the cards that would speak. Then, when the cards were spread on the table, they told me what they had to tell: that, at that moment, something ominous was happening to the things she had collected to make a home. I translated the message into words. And, it was true.

BE CAREFUL
WHAT YOU THINK
AROUND RATTLESNAKES

by J. Allen Boone

There is great practical value in carefully supervising one's thoughts and motives in contacts with other living things. Particularly with such creatures as rattlesnakes. These wise but little-understood fellows, with their poison-brewing skill and deadly defense techniques, are experts in dealing with thought emanations, especially as they come from a human.

When I first visited those parts of the West where white men and Indians frequently crossed trails with rattlesnakes, and when I had to do so myself, it was a shivery experience. I saw some of them whirl into action with their hypnotic eyes and their lightning lunges with heavily poisoned fangs. They were thorough, terrifying, and deadly killers.

One day an old desert prospector, who had had rattlesnakes as neighbors for as long as he could remember, told me a surprising thing. He said that while rattlesnakes take special delight in sinking their fangs into a white man, they seldom harm an Indian. I asked him why. He did not know, and had never tried to find out.

In my travels I found that what the old prospector had said was true. The rattlesnakes were indeed selective. They were biting the white men, and they were extending almost complete immunity to the Indians. I talked to all kinds of "snake experts," but none of them gave me a satisfying answer; certainly none gave me an answer that I would have wanted to try out on a diamond-back rattler.

Almost everywhere I went there was vicious and relentless warfare going on between white men and rattlesnakes; it was warfare to the death of either the man or the snake. But I could find no such warfare between the Indians and the rattlesnakes. There seemed to be a kind of gentlemen's agreement between them. In all my journeyings in deserts, prairies, and mountains I never once saw a rattlesnake coil, either by way of defense or attack, when an Indian walked into its close vicinity.

My experiences with the dog Strongheart* had shown me the trouble that unseen mental forces can cause in one's contacts with animals. One's thinking, in all its nakedness, always precedes him and accurately proclaims his real nature and intention. Snakes are able to detect and correctly appraise the particular kind of thinking that is moving in their direction. Having done so, they are ready to deal either as friend or as foe with the approaching human body belonging to that thinking.

What really happens when the average white man and a rattlesnake suddenly and unexpectedly meet? Having been taught to regard all snakes as loathsome and deadly enemies with no rights whatsoever on earth, the man wants to kill every snake he sees. Something intensely emotional, savage, and violent begins churning within him, filling him with repugnance, horror, and alarm. At the same time all sorts of malevolent factors latent in his nature flare up and thoroughly poison his state of mind. This invisible weapon, this deadly thought-thing, he focuses upon the rattlesnake with lethal intent.

Highly sensitive to this mental attack and keenly aware of its source, the rattlesnake by

* Strongheart was a highly intelligent canine movie star who had been Boone's roommate and companion for a period of months and with whom Boone had developed a telepathic relationship.

rapid thought action poisons its own state of mind and turns it toward the white man with equally malicious intent.

If the white man happens to have a material weapon and is able successfully to use it, he kills the snake's physical body. If, however, the snake manages to avoid the blow and gets within range, it buries its well-poisoned fangs in some part of the white man's body, and the man keeps the rendezvous with death. While the snake may victoriously jab its fangs into the white man's body, what it really strikes at is the unsocial and deadly thinking that animates the body.

Watching a real American Indian walk into the vicinity of this same rattlesnake, you would witness something entirely different. For one thing you would be unable to detect the least sign of fear or hostility in either one. As they came fairly close, you would see them pause, calmly contemplate each other for a few minutes in the friendliest fashion, then move on their respective ways again, each attending strictly to his own business and extending the same privilege to the other. During that pause between them they were in understanding communication with each other, like a big and a small ship at sea exchanging friendly messages.

Could you look deep into the thinking and motives of the Indian, you would discover the simple secret of it all, for you would find that he was moving as best he knew how in conscious rhythm with what he reverently called The Big Holy, the great primary Principle of all life, which creates and animates all things and speaks wisdom through each one of them all the time. Because of this universally operating Law, the Indian was in silent and friendly communion with the big rattler not as "a snake" that had to be feared and destroyed, but as a much-admired and much-loved "younger brother" who was entitled to as much life, liberty, happiness, respect, and consideration as he hoped to enjoy himself. His "younger brother" had reacted accordingly.

"YES, WE HAVE THE BODY"

by Elaine Hamilton

It was a late summer day in 1902 in Bowling Green, Kentucky, and the phone at Potter's Bookstore was ringing.

"Do you have a clerk there named Edgar Cayce? If so, there's a long-distance call for him from Hopkinsville."

Cayce (pronounced "Casey") hurried to the phone. Hopkinsville was his hometown, and he thought his father might be calling, or perhaps his fiancée, Gertrude Evans.

Instead the caller introduced himself as C. H. Dietrich, former superintendent of schools in Hopkinsville. "Are you familiar with the case of our daughter Aime?" he asked.

"I think so," said Cayce. "She had grippe

16

about three years ago, when she was two."

"That's right. It left her brain permanently damaged, the doctors say, and she will have the mentality of a two-year-old all her life. But lately her condition has gotten even worse — she has begun to have convulsions. Would you try to help her?"

"Well . . . ," said Cayce, hesitantly.

"We've heard about the miracles you've performed for some other people who were hopelessly ill. Your friend Al Layne, here in Hopkinsville, says you just go to sleep and then tell what's wrong with the patient and how it can be cured. At first we thought it sounded crazy, but now we're so desperate we'll try anything."

Dietrich went on to say that there was a paid ticket waiting for Cayce at the railroad station, and he begged the young man to come. Cayce, who had never been able to refuse a plea for help, took the next train to Hopkinsville.

When he reached the Dietrich home he found his "conductor," Al Layne, already there waiting for him. Layne was an amateur hypnotist and student of mail-order courses in osteopathic medicine. His goal in life was to become a doctor of osteopathy, but so far he hadn't been able to scrape up enough money to go to medical school.

As always when he was about to give a

"reading," as Layne called it, Cayce was painfully aware of the risks involved. Here they were, a "freak" who gave medical diagnoses in his sleep, and a correspondence-school medical student who barely understood them. Suppose he, Cayce, should prescribe a treatment that was likely to kill the patient. Did Layne know enough to spot the danger in time?

Cayce was introduced to five-year-old Aime, who was still a beautiful little girl in spite of her sluggish movements and dull, listless gaze. "Would you like to examine her?" the parents asked him, and then exchanged shocked looks when he answered, "No, it wouldn't do any good. I don't know a thing about medicine."

He found a place where he could lie down and proceeded to remove his jacket, loosen his tie, collar, and cuffs, and undo the laces on his shoes. When he was stretched out and relaxed, Layne sat beside him with paper and pencil and gave the suggestion that he should put himself into a deep trance. Then Layne began the induction:

"You will have before you the body of Aime Dietrich, who is here in this house. You will examine this body carefully and tell me the conditions you find at the present time, giving the cause of the existing conditions, and the treatment for the cure of this body."

There was a short pause. Then Edgar began to speak in confident, authoritative tones: "Yes,

18

we have the body. The trouble is in the spine. A few days before her illness, the body slipped while getting out of a carriage and struck the base of the spine on the carriage step. This injury caused a weakness where the grippe germs could settle and cause both the mental condition and the later attacks."

As Layne scribbled furiously, Edgar went on to give detailed instructions for making delicate adjustments to Aime's spine. He said that once these had been made, she would begin to return to normal.

"Now you will no longer see this body," said Layne, closing the session. "You will wake up and feel perfectly all right."

Edgar opened his eyes and sat up. "Did you get anything?" he asked anxiously.

"We got the first hope we've had in three years," said Mr. Dietrich, as his wife smiled through her tears. "We had forgotten all about that accident Aime had on the carriage step, till you reminded us. Mr. Layne is to make the spinal adjustments, and you said you would stay and take check readings to make sure they were done exactly right."

When he heard this, Cayce was even more frightened than he had been before, because he doubted Layne's ability to make the adjustments without causing further injury. But the parents seemed to have complete faith in the reading, so Layne went ahead. After three separate adjustments and three checkups given by Edgar in his sleep, the treatment was finished. Cayce went back to Bowling Green filled with anxiety.

Five days later, when he received another long-distance telephone call, he barely had courage enough to lift the receiver. Then, "God bless you, Edgar Cayce!" he heard Dietrich's voice exclaim. "Today Aime called us by name. Her mind seems to be leaping ahead to catch up with the years she missed."

By November Aime Dietrich had practically caught up with the other children her age and was ready to start school with them. The news of her miraculous recovery spread throughout the Hopkinsville area and was written up in the newspapers, but, to Cayce's great relief, it never reached Bowling Green. There he was still able to keep up the pretense that he was just like other people. He was well liked at his job, had made many friends in the Christian Endeavor group at the church, and was hoping that soon he would have enough money to marry Gertrude and set up housekeeping with her in Bowling Green. Only once every two weeks did he have to return to acting like a freak. On alternate Sundays, Al Layne would come up from Hopkinsville on the train, with his pockets full of urgent pleas for help, and Edgar would give readings.

Edgar Cayce was not the first of his family

to possess psychic powers. His paternal grandfather was a water dowser who told many farmers in the county just where to dig to bring in the best well. He could also make a heavy table rise into the air just by placing his fingers on it, or make a broom on the other side of the room come away from the wall and dance. After his death, Grandpa appeared several times to Edgar as the boy played alone in the yard, and the two had long talks.

Edgar had invisible playmates, too — invisible, that is, to everyone but himself and his mother. He confided in her, but he learned very early that it was best not to mention his strange experiences to his father. Leslie B. Cayce, who had the honorary title of Squire because he had once served as Justice of the Peace, was quick to scoff at such "hogwash." Yet, the day was coming when Squire Cayce would stop scoffing and start bragging about Edgar's ability to "see things."

In school Edgar was an indifferent pupil, to put it mildly. He daydreamed the hours away. His mind was a sieve — one minute he would seem to know something and the next it would be gone. For the Squire, it was a humiliation and a disgrace to have such a dimwitted son.

One day he sat Edgar down at home in front of an open spelling book. "You are going to learn to spell these words, or else," he declared. Edgar tried his best to concentrate. He

21

found that if he repeated one word over and over, he could spell it. But if he studied two more words and then came back to the first one, it was as if he had never seen it. For three hours the Squire tried to pound the lesson into Edgar's head. He raged and thundered. He tested Edgar again and again on the same words, but the boy still got them wrong.

Finally, left alone, Edgar laid his head down wearily on the spelling book and went to sleep. When he woke up he felt different. He thought he might — he was sure he did — know those words. When his father returned, Edgar handed him the speller. "Ask me any word in the book," he said. To the Squire's amazement, Edgar spelled every one perfectly, even the words in lessons he had not yet studied. Then he began to tell his father what page each word was on and what the picture on that page looked like.

After that, Edgar began to apply the same "study method" to all his other school subjects, and soon found himself at the head of the class.

It was not long after this great academic triumph that Edgar had an accident that was to change his life. It was almost as if the strange power he possessed was trying to teach him a better use to put it to than spelling and math.

While playing outdoors with some other students at recess time, Edgar was struck on the spine by a baseball. He didn't seem to be hurt much, and went back to his classes when the bell rang. Soon, however, he began acting peculiar. Where he had always been quiet and self-contained, he suddenly became noisy. He threw things, talked loudly out of turn, and picked fights with the other children. On his way home after school he rolled in mud puddles and several times jumped into the road right in front of a team of horses. At home he grabbed a pan of coffee beans that his mother was roasting, ran out into the yard with it, and planted the beans in the ground. As soon as the Squire arrived home, he put the boy forcibly to bed where, after a brief struggle, he sank into a coma.

Then, to his parents' surprise, he began to speak. "A baseball struck my spine, causing shock to the nervous system," he said. "Make a poultice of herbs and chopped raw onions, and put it at the base of my brain." He went on to name the herbs that were to be used, while his mother and father stood paralyzed with astonishment. "Hurry up," he warned them sharply, "or there will be permanent damage to the brain."

They mixed the poultice and applied it according to his instructions. Edgar fell into a normal sleep, and the next morning he was himself again.

As an adult, Cayce had many occasions to

prescribe his own treatment while in the trance state. Every time he made up his mind that he would stop giving readings and concentrate on making a good living for himself and Gertrude, he would lose his voice. He would say something like, "I'm tired of having everyone think I'm a freak or a quack or a cheap stage magician. I didn't ask God for this power, and I'm not going to use it anymore." The next statement after that would come out in a croak or a raspy whisper. When this happened, the only thing to do was to find someone who could guide him into a trance and then suggest that his body heal itself by causing the blood to flow more vigorously through his throat. On waking up, he would again be able to speak in a clear, strong voice. It was Al Layne, the amateur hypnotist, who helped Edgar discover this cure, and that was how Layne became Edgar's "conductor" in those early years in Hopkinsville.

In later years Edgar Cayce worked with a succession of qualified doctors who would write down and interpret the readings. He also insisted that each treatment recommended in the readings be carried out by a licensed practitioner. However, it was often difficult or even impossible for a patient to find a doctor who would take the reading seriously. Cayce kept getting letters that said, "I took your reading to Dr. X and he refused even to look at it."

"My doctor told me I was a fool to believe what some nutty psychic says." "The hospital assures me that the treatment you recommended would kill me." Yet, whenever a doctor could be persuaded to follow a reading, the patient always improved or recovered, even if his case had been given up as hopeless.

One such "hopeless" case involved Cayce's own son Hugh Lynn. The Cayces were living in Selma, Alabama, at the time, and Edgar was supporting the family by running a photography studio. While playing in the studio out of sight of his father, who was in the darkroom, Hugh Lynn decided to see what would happen if he piled some flash-powder on the floor and touched a lighted match to it. What happened, of course, was a terrific explosion that tore into the boy's face and blinded him.

The doctors took one look at the screaming child and shook their heads. There was hardly any hope of restoring the sight in one eye, they said; the other would have to be removed immediately to save Hugh Lynn's life.

Grimly, Cayce told them to do nothing until he had taken a reading. When it was over the doctors seemed impressed by the knowledge it revealed, but very skeptical about the treatment. While in trance, Edgar had said that Hugh Lynn would recover his sight if he was kept in a dark room for fifteen days, with dressings soaked in strong tannic acid on his eyes. "But that," protested the eye specialists, "might irreparably damage the tissues of the eye."

"Of which eye?" asked Cayce. "The one that's permanently blind or the one you want to take out anyway?"

They followed the instructions of the reading for fifteen days, during which time Hugh Lynn felt no pain whatever. When the dressings were removed, the facial skin showed only faint traces of scar tissue and the eyes were clear. Hugh Lynn gave a shout of joy. "I can see! I can see just as well as I ever could!"

Through the years Edgar Cayce somehow found time to give thousands of readings, although, since he would never accept more than $25 for one (and always gave it free to any patient who couldn't afford to pay), he had to work at a "regular" job for most of his life. When he died in Virginia Beach, Virginia, on January 3, 1945, he left a large vault full of word-for-word transcripts of the readings. Today the Association for Research and Enlightenment, which was set up to preserve and study these records, keeps Edgar Cayce's work alive through its continuing educational programs.

THE GHOST THAT STUMBLED

by Harry Price

My first "ghost" was made of cardboard. I will hasten to explain that it was the "property" specter of a three-act psychic play, "The Skeptic," which I wrote and produced when I was still a schoolboy (1898). Of course I took the leading role myself, and I am sure I played it with considerable verve!

The reason I mention my early attempt at portraying the supernatural is that "The Skeptic" was the dramatized record of a remarkable experience I had when I investigated my first haunted house.

I spent nearly all my school holidays in a little English village which I will call Parton Magna. The old Manor House in Parton

27

Magna, built around 1600 A.D., had been bought by a retired canon of the Church of England and his wife. There were rumors that the place was haunted — but popular tradition provides a ghost for every old country house, especially if a tragedy has taken place within it.

The story about the Manor House is that it was built by a rich recluse who, because of an unhappy love affair, decided to retire from the world and its disappointments. A niece looked after the old man and managed his servants. One night the recluse became suddenly demented, went to his niece's room, and strangled her. After this un-uncle-like act the old man left the house, spent the night in the neighboring woods, and at daybreak threw himself into the river that runs through the fields near the house. As with most traditions, there is a grain of truth in the story, the fact being that many years previously a girl named Mary Hulse had died at the Manor under suspicious circumstances.

The first indication the canon had that the house was haunted was a soft pattering sound, as of a child's bare feet running up and down the wide passage or gallery. Then the maids started complaining that the kitchen utensils were being disturbed. Pots and pans would fall off shelves for no apparent reason when a maid was within a few feet of them, but always when her back was turned. During the night, fires were often raked out of the fireplaces. The danger of fire from this cause was so obvious that before going to bed the canon's wife had water poured on the dying embers.

The canon's health was beginning to suffer from the anxiety caused by these disturbing events. What really drove the family out was the fact that the noises were becoming louder. A steady thump, thump, thump (as of someone in heavy boots stamping about the house) was disturbing their sleep night after night. At length they were persuaded to leave the house for at least a short period. This was in the early autumn.

On my way back to school for the Michaelmas term, I broke my journey at Parton Magna to stay a few days with friends, who told me about the state of affairs at the Manor House. I decided I would investigate, and invited another boy to join me in the adventure.

Permission to spend a night in the Manor was easily obtained from the woman (who lived in a cottage near the house) who was looking after the place, and doubtless she regarded us as a couple of mad schoolboys.

I must confess that I hadn't the slightest idea what we were going to do, or what I ought to take with me in the way of equipment. But that last question was very soon settled, because all I had with me was a quarter-plate Lancaster stand camera. On the morning of the adventure I cycled into the nearest town and bought some magnesium powder, a doorbell switch, a hank of insulated electrical wire, two Daniell's batteries, and some sulphuric acid. A big hole was made in my term's pocket money! In the afternoon I assembled my batteries and switch and prepared the flashpowder by means of which I hoped to photograph — *something!* So that there should be no unwillingness on the part of the magnesium to "go off" at the psychological moment, I extracted the white smokeless gunpowder from four or five shotgun cartridges and mixed it with the magnesium powder. By a lucky chance I had with me a delicate chemical balance which I was taking back to school. With the weights was a short piece of platinum wire which I inserted in the electrical circuit in order to ignite the magnesium flash-powder.

With the abovementioned impedimenta, a box of matches, some candles, a stable lantern, a piece of chalk, a ball of string, a box of rapid photographic plates, and a parcel of food, we bade a tender farewell to our friends and made our way across the fields to the Manor House, where we arrived at about 9:30 p.m.

The Manor House was built for comfort. From the large hall a wide staircase leads to a landing. At the top of the stairs (of which there are about fifteen — but I am speaking from memory) is, or was, a solid oak gate placed across to prevent dogs from roaming over the whole house. The staircase leads to the more important rooms opening out of a short gallery.

The first thing we did when we reached our destination was to search every room and attic, and close and fasten every window. We locked all the interior doors that could be locked, and removed the keys. The doors leading to the outside were locked, bolted, and barred, and chairs or other obstacles were piled in front of them. We then established ourselves in the morning-room, locked the door, and waited for something — or somebody — to turn up. Our only light came from the stable lantern, which we placed on the table.

At about half-past eleven, when we were beginning to get very sleepy and wishing we were in our nice, warm beds, my friend thought he heard a noise in the room overhead — the traditional room of the unfortunate Mary Hulse. I, too, heard a noise, but thought it was caused by a mouse or the wind. A few minutes later there was a thud in the room above which left nothing to the imagination. It sounded as if someone had stumbled over a chair. For a moment or so we were almost paralyzed with fear. But, remembering what we were there for, we braced up our nerves and waited.

Just before midnight we again heard a

noise in the room above; it was as if a heavy person were stamping around in clogs. A minute or so later the footfalls sounded as if they had left the room and were traversing the short gallery. Then they approached the head of the stairs, paused at the dog-gate (which we had securely fastened with string), and commenced descending the stairs. We distinctly counted fifteen thumps, corresponding to the number of stairs — and I need hardly mention that our hearts were thumping in unison.

"It" seemed to pause in the hall when the bottom of the stairs was reached, and we were wondering what was going to happen next. We were not kept long in suspense. The entity, having paused in the hall for about three minutes, turned and stumped up the stairs again. We again counted the number of thumps, and were satisfied that "it" was at the top of the flight, at the dog-gate. No further noise was heard when this gate had been reached.

My friend and I waited at the door for a few minutes more, and then we decided to investigate the neighborhood of the dog-gate and Mary Hulse's room. But we had barely formed this resolution before we heard the thumps descending the stairs again. With quickened pulse I again counted the fifteen heavy footsteps, which were getting nearer and nearer and louder and louder. There was another pause in the hall, and again the footfalls started their upward journey.

By this time the excitement of the adventure was making us bolder. We decided to have a look at our quarry, if it was visible, so with my courage in one hand and the camera in the other, I opened the door. My friend was close behind with the lantern. By this time the "ghost" was on about the fifth stair, but with the opening of the door the noise of its ascent stopped dead.

Realizing that the ghost was as frightened of meeting us as we were of seeing it (although that was what we had come for), we thought we would again examine the stairs and the upper part of the house. This we did very thoroughly, but found nothing disturbed. The dog-gate was still latched and tied with string. We were disappointed at not seeing anything we could photograph, so decided to make an attempt at a flashlight picture if the ghost would descend the stairs again.

For my stand for the flash-powder I used a household stepladder about six feet high which we found in the kitchen. I opened out the stepladder and placed it about twelve feet from the bottom of the stairs. On the top of the ladder in an old watch-case I placed a heaped-up eggcupful of the magnesium-gunpowder mixture — enough to photograph every ghost in the county! I placed the two Daniell's batteries in the morning-room, and, with the electrical wire, connected the batteries to the magnesium powder on the ladder and the doorbell switch, which I had placed on the floor of the morning-room, the wire entering the room under the door. In the heap of powder I had buried the platinum wire, which was interposed in the electrical circuit.

The exact position where we should photograph the entity presented some difficulty. We were not sure what happened to it when it reached the hall, so we decided to make an attempt at photographing it when it was ascending or descending the stairs. We decided to try during the ascent, arguing (which shows how simple we were!) that the ghost would have become less suspicious of us by the time it was on its return journey! I stationed my friend on the seventh or eighth stair (I forget which), and he held a lighted match which I accurately focused on the ground-glass [view-finder] of my camera, which I placed on one of the treads of the stepladder. I inserted the photographic plate, withdrew the flap, uncapped the lens, and all was ready.

By this time, it was about half-past one. We returned to the morning-room, locked the door again, and extinguished the lantern.

It must have been nearly an hour before we heard anything, and again it was from the

Mary Hulse room that the noise came. Shortly after, the thumps could be heard approaching the dog-gate and again "it" paused at the top of the stairs. It passed over — or through — the dog-gate and commenced stumping down the stairs again. Having reached the hall it stopped, and in my mind's eye I could picture it examining the arrangements we had made for securing its photograph. Then we thought we heard the stepladder moved. In order to get the camera square with the stairs I had taken a large book — using it as a T-square — and drawn on the tiled floor a chalk line parallel with the stairs. Exactly against this line I had placed the two front feet of the stepladder.

During the next five or six minutes we heard no movement in the hall. Then suddenly "it" started its return journey. With our hearts beating wildly, we lay on the floor counting the slow, measured thumps as they ascended the stairs. At the seventh thump I pressed the bell switch — and a most extraordinary thing happened. At the moment of the explosion the ghost was so startled *that it involuntarily stumbled* on the stairs, as we could plainly hear, and then there was silence.

We opened the door and found the hall filled with a dense white smoke in which we could hardly breathe. We re-capped the camera, relit our lantern, and made a tour of inspection. The first thing we noticed was that the stepladder was shifted slightly out of the square. Whether "it" moved the ladder (as we thought at the time) or the shock of the explosion was responsible (which is doubtful), we could not determine.

We immediately developed the plate, but nothing but an over-exposed picture of the staircase was on the negative.

The Manor House continued to be the center of psychic activity for some months after our curious adventure, but the disturbances became gradually less frequent, and eventually ceased. Fate decreed that some years later I should spend very many happy weeks in the house. If sometimes during that period my heart beat faster than its accustomed rate, the cause was *not* a supernatural one! Suffice it to say that I did not see or hear anything of the alleged spirit of Mary Hulse, though I will candidly admit that I was not looking for her — my interest in the diaphanous maiden having been transferred by that time to one of a much more objective nature!

THE MOST HAUNTED HOUSE IN ENGLAND

by Marie Norel

What caused the strange happenings at Borley Rectory in Sussex, England, remains a mystery to this day. But the rector himself saw the ghostly coach and horses, driven by a headless coachman, lurch past him on a country road at night. And other things, nearly as strange, were reported by more than a hundred skeptical observers during the years between 1929 and 1939.

Sometime after the rector had moved out of Borley Rectory, Harry Price, a psychic researcher, took on the job of finding out just what was going on, and why. Price went about his task very scientifically. Included in the paraphernalia he took with him to Borley were: a camera and flash bulbs, a remote-control movie camera, a bowl of mercury to detect tremors in rooms or passageways; and tape and lead seals with which to seal doors and windows so that no human being could pass through undetected.

Price and his secretary arrived at the rectory in time for lunch on June 12, 1929. While they ate, they were given a brief history of the house by its current owner, whom Price referred to afterwards as "Mr. H. Robinson" (not his real name).

The house was built in 1863 by Thomas Percival, who died there in 1897. His son, Walter Percival, inherited the property and lived there until 1927, when he died after a long and painful illness. His death took place, it should be noted, in the Blue Room. Since then a succession of owners had occupied the mansion, but none had ever stayed for more than a few months because, they complained, it was haunted. Mr. Robinson, a levelheaded and practical man, had taken possession in the spring of 1929. Yes, he had heard about the ghosts and other disturbances, but hadn't believed a word of it.

It was a fact, however, that on the site where Borley Rectory now stood there had been, in the twelfth century, a monastery and an underground burial vault belonging to it. According to one legend, a coachman who worked at the monastery fell in love with a nun at a nearby convent. One night the couple tried to elope in a black coach drawn by two bay horses, driven by a lay brother. The three fugitives were pursued, caught, and brought back for trial and punishment. The nun was walled up alive; her lover was beheaded.

The apparition of the unfortunate nun had appeared to so many people on the lawn at Borley Rectory that the path where she was most often seen had come to be called the Nun's Walk. Many people also claimed to have seen the coach and horses careening through the rectory grounds, while inside, it was said, the ghost of Walter Percival strolled about, dressed in the gray bedjacket in which he died.

But it wasn't the apparitions that were bothering the Robinson family. It was other disturbances. Bells rang at all hours of the day and night when no one was there to ring them. Door-keys began to fall out of their locks, the family replacing each one carefully, after which the keys fell out again and disappeared completely. Soft footsteps of invisible slippered feet were heard; pebbles were hurled through the air and down the staircase. By the time Price arrived on the scene, the Robinsons were almost desperate enough to move out.

After lunch on that first afternoon, Price and his secretary set to work exploring the house from top to bottom. They found nothing stranger than a few toads and newts in the cellar.

That evening in the garden, however, Price and a reporter from a London newspaper actually saw the nun. The two men had taken up their post at dusk in the doorway of a large summerhouse. They had been waiting nearly an hour when the reporter suddenly gripped Price's arm and whispered, "There she is!" Price looked toward the Nun's Walk and saw a shadowy figure gliding down the path under the trees. The reporter dashed across the lawn toward the figure. When he came back, he told Price that the figure had become more distinct as he approached it, but had "melted away" when he reached the spot.

On their way back into the house, Price and the reporter were crossing a glass-roofed porch when there was a terrific crash. A pane of glass from the roof had hurtled down and smashed just a few feet from them.

They entered the house and again searched it from cellar to roof. Just as they were coming downstairs after this investigation, a red glass candlestick holder from the Blue Room came flying down the staircase and struck an iron stove in the hall, splattering Price with splinters of glass. Immediately after that, a mothball came tumbling down the stairs. Having just searched the upper rooms, Price was convinced there was no one up there.

On that first visit to Borley Rectory, Price stayed three nights and witnessed disturbances every evening. His secretary stayed over the weekend and the phenomena continued. A week or so later, Mr. Robinson and his wife moved out of the house.

After investigating Borley Rectory off and on for a number of years, Price decided to make a thorough job of it. He rented the rectory for a year and placed an ad in the London *Times:* "Haunted House. Responsible persons of leisure and intelligence, intrepid, critical, and unbiased, are invited to join group of observers in a year's night-and-day investigation of alleged haunted house. . . ." Two hundred persons responded. Price selected 40 men and two women. They were given written instructions and were told to report anything unusual to Price.

Almost every observer at Borley reported having strange experiences. Objects moved, writing appeared on the wall, and on one occasion an investigator felt the air around him grow cold and remain so for nearly half a minute. Two dogs approached the same spot and ran away, terrified. The house certainly seemed to deserve the label Price had given it: "The most haunted house in England."

Finally the search was discontinued, and a new tenant moved into Borley Rectory. In 1939 he accidentally overturned an oil lamp, and the house was soon destroyed by the flames — fulfilling a prophecy that had been written on the wall some time earlier. Today, if the ruins of Borley Rectory are inhabited, it is entirely by ghosts.

THE GHOST IN THE BLACK LACE MANTILLA

by Eleanor Van Zandt

The old Wedderburn house in Narragansett, Rhode Island, stands overlooking the Atlantic. A long upstairs gallery, with eight tall windows, gives a wonderful view of the sea. In the 1830's, shortly after he had built the house, Captain Japhet Wedderburn brought home from one of his voyages a Spanish wife. Shortly after that, he went off on another voyage, leaving Doña Mercedes alone in the big house with only the housekeeper, Huldy, for company. The Captain was away for most of the next six years, during which time Doña Mercedes never ventured out of the house, but passed the hours walking up and down the gallery, looking out to sea and crying. She was so tiny that she

43

looked like a child dressed up in a Spanish comb and black lace mantilla. Huldy reported to a friend that her mistress kept a satchel packed at all times, ready to return to the island of Tortuga, where her family lived.

Once Huldy became ill and had to go home for three months. During this time, Japhet came back from one of his voyages. He announced he was going to take his wife with him on his next cruise, so that she could visit her family. One dark, sleety night his ship sailed away.

Two years later Japhet returned, alone. When asked about his wife, he explained that she had hated living in Narragansett, and that he had persuaded her to make a good, long visit to her family. He would bring her back on the next voyage.

But on the next voyage, Captain Wedderburn died of a heart attack.

The house was sold to a family with several children. One day the oldest daughter, just returned from boarding school, asked her mother, "Have we acquired a Spanish governess for Tommy and Beth? Who is the woman I saw in the upstairs hall?"

The mother was completely mystified, but Tommy also reported having seen the tiny figure in the black lace mantilla.

Succeeding tenants of the house also encountered the weeping, black-clad woman in the hall. Wringing her hands and pointing out to sea, she would stand there a few moments and then disappear.

Some years ago, a charitable organization bought the Wedderburn house with the purpose of turning it into a summer retreat for underprivileged city children. While repairs were in progress, workmen noticed a cracked hearthstone by one of the fireplaces. They decided to rip out the fireplace entirely. When they pried up the hearthstone, they found a small wooden coffin. Inside lay a female skeleton, its skull resting on a large tortoise-shell comb. Ragged bits of black lace still clung to it.

THE TRAVELING SALESMAN AND THE GHOST

This account was sent in 1887 to the American Society for Psychical Research by Mr. F. G. of Boston.

Sir: Replying to the recently published request of your Society for actual occurrences of psychical phenomena, I respectfully submit the following remarkable occurrence. I have never mentioned it outside of my family and a few intimate friends, knowing well that few would believe it.

In 1867 my only sister, a young lady of eighteen years, died suddenly of cholera in St. Louis, Missouri. My attachment for her was very strong, and the blow a severe one to me.

A year or so after her death I became a commercial traveler, and it was in 1876, while on one of my western trips, that the event occurred.

I had "drummed" the city of St. Joseph, Missouri, and had gone to my room at the Pacific House to send in my orders, which were unusually large ones, so that I was in a very happy frame of mind indeed. My thoughts, of course, were about these orders. I had not been thinking of my late sister, or in any manner reflecting on the past.

The hour was high noon, and the sun was shining cheerfully into my room. While busily smoking a cigar and writing out my orders, I suddenly became conscious that someone was sitting on my left, with one arm resting on the table. Quick as a flash I turned and distinctly saw the form of my dead sister, and for a brief second or so looked her squarely in the face; and so sure was I that it was she, that I sprang forward in delight, calling her by name. As I did so, the apparition instantly vanished.

Naturally I was startled and dumbfounded, almost doubting my senses. But the cigar in my mouth, the pen in my hand, and the ink still moist on my letter convinced me that I had not been dreaming and was wide awake. I was near enough to touch her, had it been a physical possibility, and noted her features, expression, and details of dress. She appeared as if alive. Her eyes looked kindly and perfectly naturally into mine. Her skin was so lifelike that I could see the glow of moisture on its surface.

This visitation, or whatever you may call it, so impressed me that I took the next train home, and in the presence of my parents and others I related what had occurred. My father, a man of rare good sense and very practical, was inclined to ridicule me. But he, too, was amazed when later on I told them of a bright red line or scratch on the right-hand side of my sister's face, which I distinctly had seen. When I mentioned this, my mother rose trembling to her feet and nearly fainted away, and as soon as she sufficiently recovered her self-possession, with tears streaming down her face, she exclaimed that I had indeed seen my sister. She said that no living mortal but herself was aware of that scratch, which she had accidentally made while doing some little act of kindness after my sister's death. She said she well remembered how pained she was to think she should have marred the features of her dead daughter, and that, unknown to all, she had carefully obliterated all traces of the slight scratch with powder. She had never mentioned it to a human being from that day to this. In proof, neither my father nor any of our family had detected it, and positively were unaware of the incident, yet *I saw the scratch as bright as if just made*.

My mother told me *she knew* at least that I had seen my sister. A few weeks later she died, happy in her belief that she would rejoin her favorite daughter in a better world.

WHAT CAUSES GHOSTS?
from *The Haunted Mind*

by Nandor Fodor

For centuries people have been trying to figure out what causes ghosts. The explanation that's probably heard most often is that nothing causes them, because ghosts don't exist. Anyone who claims to have seen a ghost must have been the victim of a prank, or was fooled by an optical illusion, or is simply fibbing.

But suppose two or more people see the ghost independently, and their reports tally? Suppose the possibility of its being a prank has been ruled out? Suppose their story, if believed, is going to cost them their home and a lot of money? In such a case, a theory that simply denies the ghost's existence doesn't help much.

So here's another: Human events that arouse strong emotions leave some kind of psychic imprint on the place where they happen. Later, sensitive persons visiting the place see the event replayed before their eyes like a movie. This theory would seem to explain why some people see the ghosts in allegedly haunted houses while others, standing right next to them, see nothing.

However, the "psychic imprint" theory doesn't quite cover the case of the Green Man of Ash Manor. The Green Man seemed to be more than just the kind of image that goes through the same motions every time the film is run. He seemed to be capable of varying his actions and also of trying to communicate with his reluctant hosts. Dr. Nandor Fodor, who investigated the Ash Manor haunting, was inclined to think that the Green Man was neither imprint nor spirit, but just a projection of part of a living person's mind. He couldn't be positive, of course; but as a psychoanalyst, he found this explanation appealing.

A fourth explanation was suggested when Dr. Fodor brought a famous medium, Mrs. Eileen Garrett, to Ash Manor in an attempt to find out what the Green Man wanted. Mrs. Garrett was what is called a spirit medium, which means that when she was in a trance her mind and body seemed to be taken over by a "spirit control," who brought messages from people who had died and "passed over." Mrs. Garrett's control was a man named Uvani, who in life had been an Arabian. Speaking through Mrs. Garrett's voice, Uvani "psychoanalyzed" the Ash Manor haunting in a way that impressed even the skeptical doctor.

Which ghostly theory is right? The "bah, humbug theory"; the psychic-imprint theory; the mental-projection theory; or Uvani's soul-in-limbo theory? As yet, none has been either proved or disproved. Still, Uvani's idea does have something to recommend it that the others don't have: Its author should have known a lot about spirits, because he was one himself.

—M.B.

THE ASH MANOR GHOST

With Excerpts from
The Haunted Mind
by Nandor Fodor

Ash Manor House, in Sussex, England, dates from the time of Edward the Confessor, King of England from 1042 to 1066. Thus, by the time it was bought in 1934 by a Mr. Keel, the house had seen enough war, pestilence, and death to generate a whole army of ghosts. Only one appeared, but that one caused such an uproar that the Keel family were on the verge of putting Ash Manor up for sale again. They had even decided they would take less money than they had paid for it, if need be. (By the way, Keel was not their real name.)

In July 1936, Dr. Nandor Fodor, a psychoanalyst, was invited to visit Ash Manor by a woman who was writing a book about haunted houses. At the time of his visit the family consisted of Mr. and Mrs. Keel and their daughter Patricia, sixteen years old. The house was being run by a butler and his wife, who had been recently hired and who were — thus far — unaware that Ash Manor had a ghost.

As the Keels explained to Dr. Fodor, the haunting had begun with the sound of footsteps in the attic. But since the attic had no floor, they knew there could be no one up there and ignored the sounds. Then one night Mr. Keel was awakened by three violent knocks on his bedroom door. The next night at the same hour (3:35 a.m.) there were two violent knocks on his door. Before the ghost could get down to one knock and then — terrifying idea — sudden entry without warning, Mr. Keel went away on business. Here is what happened on the first night of his return.

"The room was unnaturally cold and there was something unpleasant about it. I therefore decided to remain awake and see what I could see. Nothing happened until 3 a.m. Then I fell asleep. A short while later I was aroused by a violent bang on the door, which I had left open. I sat up with a jerk.

"Standing in the doorway I saw a little oldish man, dressed in a green smock, very muddy breeches and gaiters, a slouch hat on his head and a handkerchief around his neck.

"I thought that a servant had left a door

open and a tramp had walked in. I challenged him but got no reply. I demanded again what he wanted in my house, and, as he just stood stupidly staring at me, I jumped out of bed and seized him by the shoulder. My hand went right through him. I lost my balance and must have fainted from the shock.

"All I remember is that eventually I reached my wife's bedroom and there babbled so incoherently that she ran back along the passage to get some brandy.

"The ghost still stood at my bedroom door and she also mistook it for a tramp. When it would not answer or move, she hit out with her clenched fist — and bruised her hand against the lintel of the door. It went clean through. She turned and ran.

"Remember, I had no chance of telling her what I had seen, yet her description exactly coincided with mine."

Mrs. Keel gave Dr. Fodor the following testimony:

"We saw Ash Manor House for the first time in the summer of 1933. The bedroom which is haunted was then used by the servants. As it was the only decent bedroom in the house, I wondered why this should be.

"We bought the house in June 1934. The owner asked a sum that we could not afford. When we stated this, the price was instantly dropped to a surprising extent. I thought that there must be trouble with the drains or with the roof. But we found everything all right.

"At the time of taking the house, the haunted bedroom was empty. The owner told me that the servants who used it ran away in the middle of the night, and it had not been used since. I still suspected the roof and not the room. For some reason I could never go into that room. But when I did for the first time, after we bought the house, I admit I did not like the feeling of it.

"My husband has an extremely material outlook. He never believed in anything supernormal and would not have taken any notice of such idle tales even if ghosts had been mentioned. He sleeps very heavily and, as a rule, nothing on earth can wake him once he is off. He has notes of the exact dates when things began to happen.

"The first thing that happened was three terrific knocks on his door. That woke up everybody in the house. No cause has been found for these knocks. No one admitted responsibility for them. Next night the knocks came again, this time only two. I believe the date was November 1934.

"For two or three nights nothing happened. My husband was away. I saw that he was nervous when he came back, but he would not admit it. I could see from my room at the end of the corridor that he was reading in bed until about three o'clock. This is the usual hour for the visitation. At three o'clock he put out his light.

"Twenty minutes later there was a heavy fall, an appalling scream, my husband ran into my room and collapsed in a dead faint. His face was livid, his eyes were bulging, and terror was written over every line of his countenance.

"There was an uproar in the house. Everybody came running into my room. My husband was still unconscious. I was afraid he was going to die. I wanted to give him some brandy. So I ran into the servants' bedroom (*i.e., the "haunted" room, now empty*), where the keys of the wine cellar were kept. I did not stop to put on the light. I tore along the passage and got the keys.

"Coming out of the room, I stopped for a second to find the step in the gloom. The servants' bedroom is almost alongside my husband's but is set in deeper and there is a small passage in front of it. It is one step higher than the landing with the staircase. I was looking for this step to avoid falling, and, as my eyes were searching the ground, I saw a man's feet and leggings in the doorway of my husband's bedroom. I looked up and there was the figure of a little man, very solid, absolutely clear. It did not occur to me, or to my husband until the next day, that there must have been something strange about this visibility. The figure did not emit light. There was no aura around it. Yet it was not only distinct but it impressed every single feature of its appearance with a startling vividity on my mind.

"He had an old smock on, Elizabethan leggings and boots covered with clay or mud. There was a red handkerchief around the neck, the chin was clean-shaven but there was hair under it. He wore a pudding basin hat, little and round. His face was very red, the eyes malevolent and horrid, the mouth open and dribbling. He stared at me with the look of an idiot.

"I thought that someone had broken into the house and was playing a practical joke on my husband. I faced him angrily: 'What do you want? Who are you?'

"Not for a moment did it occur to me that the figure was an apparition. It was as solid as any being of flesh could be. He did not answer my question and I tried to hit him with the full force of my fist.

"My hand went right through and was cut to ribbons on the lintel of the door. The force of the blow and the pain sent me spinning around. There, as I stopped, was the little man, as solid and immovable as before.

"I want you to realize that my husband, still in a dead faint in my room, had not told me a word of what he saw. I was totally unprepared for what happened. Yet my description of the apparition coincides fully with what he saw. In fact, he did the very thing that I did. He challenged the Green Man and hit him. His fist also went through him. The fall which I heard was due to the impetus behind the blow. He could not help crashing.

"I now realized that something not of this world was abroad. It was a dreadful moment. I turned and fled down the stairs into the cellar.

"The full story of the night was not revealed to me until my husband came to. As both of us, unknown to each other, had the same experience and our description of the figure coincided to minute details, there was no room for hallucination or self-deception.

"We realized that our house was haunted. We knew now why our servants refused to stay and, on inquiring in the village, we found out that the house had a bad reputation. People were not communicative and would say nothing, except that none would spend a night in 'that house' for a hundred pounds. It was 'haunted.'

"As a rule, I do not like talking to people about our experience. I have a feeling as if a share of personal responsibility were attached to us. The previous owner had the house for seven years. Before him, an elderly couple lived in it for thirteen years. They were never disturbed. Did we, in some manner, bring the haunting about?

"We saw the Green Man altogether about two dozen times. We hear him more often. Footsteps and knocks. In olden days the servants slept in the attic. But there are no floor boards there now. Only the joists are left. You cannot walk heavily on the joists. Yet we hear the footsteps as if the old boards were still in their place. The Green Man now also walks around my husband's room. He seems to appear from the wall of ten-foot-wide chimney on the landing. He goes into the bedroom and disappears through the other end of the chimney! There is a small cupboard there which once belonged to the chimney. We suspect that it was, until opened, a priest hole [a hiding place for priests in the days when Roman Catholicism was outlawed in England]; also that it communicated with the inside of the chimney. We know there is a ladder inside the chimney or steps to allow mounting but we have never seen it.

"When the Green Man appears, my husband calls for me. I go into his room and touch the ghost with an extended finger. That makes it vanish. At first, he just vanished into thin air. Lately, he retreats into the cupboard and is gone. That makes me suspect that the solution of the mystery is between the point of the Green Man's emergence and disappearance, i.e., in the chimney. I would not be surprised if, on opening it, we discovered a skeleton.

"The man, a farm laborer by his appearance, must have been murdered. The third time when I saw him, he deliberately raised his head. I saw a cut all around his neck. Something horrible was sticking out, like a cut windpipe and a mass of things with jagged edges. I cannot help feeling that the Green Man comes to call attention to an ancient murder and that, perhaps, he wants to be decently buried. I feel very sorry for him.

"Our doors have wooden latches and a wooden bolt inside. If you shut this bolt into place, the door cannot be opened from the outside. One night (this was the only occasion when we had trouble outside the haunted bedroom and the landing) heavy, crashing footsteps came down the corridor toward my bedroom. I thought it was my husband who was coming. But I got a queer feeling as I looked at the dog. He was frightfully agitated.

"The door was locked, yet it flew open and, in good electric light in the presence of my daughter and myself, an invisible man went across the room.

"Clamp, clamp, clamp . . . the footsteps crossed the room. The sound of them was in no way softened when the invisible man crossed the carpet. Followed by the eyes of my terrified dog, whose every hair stood up on its body, the sound rose in the air as if the ghost was mounting an invisible wooden staircase, then the trapdoor flew up and the footsteps continued in the attic.

"We asked the previous owner of the house if there had been a staircase in my room. He admitted that there had been. He had it taken away because he built a fireplace in the exact spot.

"I cannot explain why the Green Man's appearance should leave such a vivid impression on the mind. It would be impossible to see him so clearly in electric light as we have seen him in darkness. I could see the texture of his skin, the weatherbeaten, rugged lines of his face. Judging by the costume, I would say that the man lived 100–150 years ago. It is impossible to go back so far in the history of the house.

"As I had the suspicion that the chimney held human remains, we once had it opened. But the builder only cut a peephole. We shall have to have it opened again and allow a man to enter and explore. Most of the fireplaces of the house converge on this huge chimney.

"I had a priest in who blessed the house. It made things worse. For two nights I knelt outside my door praying and fighting some tangible force of evil. I have never been so frightened in my life. It was as if some invisible power tried to hypnotize me. I felt enclosed from every side by evil and almost succumbed.

"Two other, not ecclesiastical, exorcists also tried to help. They helped themselves, by a substantial fee, more than they helped us. They said that the house was built on a Druid circle, and that the priestly exorcism provoked this ancient evil."

July 22, 1936   (signed) Katherine Keel

"I testify that the above statement is in full agreement with the facts as known to me from my own experience and from my wife's account as given to me immediately after."

July 22, 1936   (signed) M. Keel

"I have been with Mother in her room when the invisible footsteps crossed it. Mother's statements regarding the details are correct."

July 22, 1936   (signed) Pat Keel

On July 25, Dr. Fodor brought the noted medium Eileen Garrett to Ash Manor. At 9 p.m. that evening Mrs. Garrett conducted a séance in the haunted room.

She went into a trance. Then she stirred, crossed her arms over her chest, bowed deeply, and addressed the company in the quaint accents of her Arabian spirit control, Uvani:

"It is I, Uvani, I give you greeting."

Dr. Fodor returned the greeting and explained that the house was disturbed by a ghostly visitation. The owners felt that the ghost was suffering intensely and they were upset. "Is it possible to do something for them and the ghost?"

Uvani answered:

"You will not mind if I say that where there is unhappiness in a house and there is an impression of someone coming back it is because you make for that spirit a Garden of Memory in which it can live and revive its sufferings. Unless you are, consciously or unconsciously, in a state of mind in which this impression can vivify itself, you will not be troubled. Haven't you discovered that these things only happen to you when you are in a bad emotional state, physically or mentally disturbed? Don't you realize that you yourself vivify this memory?"

Dr. Fodor objected that the ghost must be something more than a memory, because it seemed to be quite solid. Uvani replied:

"Isn't there a picture that belongs to the original frame? Life cannot die. You can explode its dynamism but you cannot dissipate its energy. If you suffer where life suffered, the essence that once filled the frame will take from you something to dramatize and live again. A sensitive person may easily vivify not one, but a thousand memories. About 500 yards to the west of this house there was, in the early part of the fifteenth century, a temporary jail for prisoners of state.

Many men and women lost their lives there. There are dozens of unhappy souls about. If a particular one comes to trouble you, it is because that one has an affinity with you. If you are nervously depleted and live in this room, you give out energy with which the ghost builds itself up like a picture on the stage."

When asked how the haunting could be cured, Uvani said he would stand aside and allow the ghost to take possession of "this instrument," by which he meant the medium's body. He told Dr. Fodor to "wake the ghost up," to tell the Green Man that he had no business in this place and time and that he should go away and leave them in peace.

Mrs. Garrett then underwent a remarkable change in appearance. The ghost had apparently taken over, for, on looking closely at Mrs. Garrett, both Mr. and Mrs. Keel gasped and said she was the very image of the Green Man.

First "he" felt his neck, tapped his lips, and tried to speak, without success. Then he beckoned for Dr. Fodor to come near, and when the doctor did so, the ghost grabbed his left hand and held it in a grip like a vise. Kneeling before the doctor, whom he evidently took to be his jailor, he cried out for mercy, using the word *eleison*, from a church prayer, and pronouncing it in the medieval fashion. When Dr. Fodor assured him that he was among friends who wanted to help him, the Green Man began to rail against his enemies. He begged the doctor to help him avenge himself on Buckingham, who had apparently stolen his wife, and the Earl of Huntingdon, who had taken his lands. Dr. Fodor replied that it was his passionate desire for vengeance that was keeping him in this earthly prison. He promised the ghost that if he would cease hating he could be reunited with his wife and son. The ghost agreed, and the séance ended on a hopeful note.

However, the next night the Green Man was back, evidently dissatisfied with the bargain he had made. He stood in Mr. Keel's doorway and tried to speak, but without the help of Mrs. Garrett's vocal cords he could not make a sound.

Two days later, Dr. Fodor again made contact with the ghost through Mrs. Garrett, this time at her home. The Green Man said he had seen his son but not his wife, and he wanted to know where she was. He reproached Dr. Fodor for not having been at Ash Manor when he returned, "though you promised to stand by me."

Then Uvani took over to explain:

"Let me, first of all, take away from you the feeling of personal responsibility. You could not definitely know whether you had the serious cooperation of your host and hostess. They were interested, but they were also very frightened. They did not, for one moment, believe that you could bring the ghost to life. They were not ready for what happened. They did not even desire to help you.

"They have used this poor, unhappy creature over a period of months to embarrass each other. They provided an atmosphere in which this unhappy one could express himself. Take the ghost away from your hosts, and you take away something with which they have been able to make both friends and enemies.

"I am concerned only with them because of the unhappy situation they created in that house. The time will come when they will give up the house. But if they continue to supply the atmosphere that they do at present, they will make the house haunted and unhappy for future tenants."

Later, in separate talks with Mr. and Mrs. Keel, Dr. Fodor learned that Uvani was right. The family was being torn apart by conflicts between husband and wife and between mother and daughter. Mr. Keel admitted that he was the source of most of the conflict and that, furthermore, he had not really wanted the ghost to be exorcized. Now that his twisted feelings had been exposed, however, Mr. Keel realized how close to insanity they had brought him.

Whether the Green Man was the surviving

spirit of a dead man, or a projection from the mind of a living one, the solution appeared to be the same: Mr. Keel must let the ghost go. He did so, and the Green Man was never seen at Ash Manor again.

The Ghost's Lament

Woe's me, woe's me,
The acorn's not yet
Fallen from the tree
That's to grow the wood,
That's to make the cradle,
That's to rock the baby,
That's to grow a man,
That's to release me.

—English folk ballad

POLTERGEISTS

Poltergeists seem to have been around since the beginning of history, but they seem to have had their impressive-sounding name only since the time of the Protestant Reformation in Germany. Martin Luther himself used the term, which means in German "noisy, racketing spirit."

Typically, a poltergeist disturbance involves two types of event: (1) rappings, tappings, thumps, buzzings, and other noises whose causes cannot be discovered; and (2) the movement of objects by some invisible force.

If the moving objects are small, they often seem to float through the air, going much more slowly than they would if they had been thrown in the ordinary way. Sometimes they even turn corners. If the objects are large — bookcases and dressers, for example — they may lift off gently like silent rockets and glide across the room. Usually these flying and dancing objects act as if they were under orders not to actually hurt any human being, though scaring the victim stiff is allowed and even encouraged. Thus, a dish may be hurled at somebody, but only graze his ear on the way to smashing itself to smithereens against the wall.

Of course, there have been poltergeists that didn't obey orders. One resident of Borley Rectory, a woman who moved in shortly after Harry Price's 1929 investigation, was nearly smothered by the mattress on her bed.

Other kinds of mischief that poltergeists occasionally get into include lighting fires; picking people up and carrying them around; pushing and pulling them; biting and pinching them; writing on the wall; and even talking (generally in shockingly bad language).

Whatever its favorite hobby, however, the average poltergeist likes to hang around a house where there is a young person. Often an adolescent girl or boy seems to be the focus of the activities; when the focus leaves the house, the disturbances either cease or follow him or her to the new location. This fact has led some psychic researchers to wonder whether the energy to perform the strange feats might not come from the unconscious mind of the focus. Another theory is that something in the young person's unconscious mind may act to trigger psychic energy in the surrounding atmosphere.

—M.B.

THINGS THAT GO "BUMP" IN THE NIGHT

by Margaret Ronan

The Lynch farm near Menomonie, Wisconsin, wasn't the most exciting place in the world to live. In fact, life there could be downright dull. In fact, it *was* dull — until one summer morning when the Lynch family sat down to breakfast and their lives took a sharp turn for the bizarre.

Breakfast never did get eaten that morning. Before the family's astonished eyes, fried eggs rose from the plates, sailed through the air, and splattered against the walls. Coffee cups overturned themselves, and pancakes were flung on the floor by unseen hands. Then came a sound like that of rapidly moving scissor blades, and 12-year-old Rena Lynch screamed as her long hair was snipped off cleanly and let drop to the floor.

More mischief followed. A new dress belonging to Mrs. Lynch disappeared for a day, only to reappear hanging in the barn, cut down and resewn to fit a child. A bowl of homemade soap wandered from room to room. Pots and pans bounced about the kitchen. The unfortunate Lynches seemed to be playing host to a poltergeist.

Poltergeist is a German word that means noise-making ghost. Unlike your common, garden-variety ghost, poltergeists are never seen. But they are certainly heard, and often felt, too. They're the practical jokers of the spirit world, the cut-ups, the hams. The Lynches' poltergeist was such a ham that it performed night and day, and before long sightseers were arriving from far and near to see the ghostly goings-on. Spook and sightseers finally drove the exhausted family to give up their farm and move away.

Should your home ever become a happy haunting ground, you might take a tip from the Swiss. There's a haunted house on Junkerngasse in Bern. For a long time no one would live in this house because it was full of the sounds of slamming doors, running footsteps, and eerie laughter. But the thrifty Bernese had no intention of letting a well-built dwelling stand empty just because it was haunted, so they put it to use as a storehouse for the local police records. Not surprisingly, the turnover of employees in the archives is heavy. "It's impossible to concentrate," complained one woman who left her job there after three months. "All day long, footsteps ran past my door, but there was never a soul in sight."

One of the best documented poltergeist cases in recent times took place in the four-room apartment of Mrs. Maybelle Clark in Newark, New Jersey, in 1961. It began on the 13th birthday of her grandson, Ernest Rivers, who lived with her. As the boy sat doing his homework, a pepper shaker floated off a shelf, described a circle in the air, and landed beside him.

But that was only the beginning. For the next two weeks, wherever Ernest went in the apartment, the crockery followed. Dishes whizzed by his head, a lamp jumped off a table and smashed at his feet, glasses left the kitchen drainboard and smashed to bits *in the air* as he passed by.

The breaking point came when a five-pound electric iron sailed through Mrs. Clark's bedroom, its cord streaming behind like the tail of a comet. Visitors began to crowd into the apartment to see the poltergeist at work. Mrs. Clark, unable to bear any more breakage, appealed for help. It came from Dr. Charles Wrege, an assistant professor of management

75

psychology at New York University's School of Management.

Dr. Wrege settled down at the apartment, investigating every object in every room to be sure there was no trickery. He was soon convinced that Ernest was exerting no physical force to make the objects move. During Wrege's "stakeout," a large crowd gathered outside the building to "see the boy who makes things fly." Police arrived to disperse the crowds, and at that moment a saltcellar came flying in from the kitchen, grazing Ernest's head.

That saltcellar was the last thing the Clark poltergeist threw. Perhaps all the visitors frightened it away. But the Clark case will go down in psychic research history because it was the first case ever reported from a housing development, with all the unwelcome activity centering in only one small apartment in a large complex of buildings.

Some scientists believe that poltergeist disturbances may be caused by the movement of water in underground streams and rivers. According to their theory, a sudden increase in volume of the water results in compression of the air. In turn, this compressed air sets up vibrations capable of shaking the foundations of houses, and may even cause doors to open and shut, window glass to crack, furniture to slide about, and objects to fall off shelves. They say that the underground water can also make weird and frightening noises, especially in old houses with basement wells.

It is possible that water-caused tremors could have had something to do with the activities of the poltergeist in the home of James Herrmann in Seaford, Long Island, New York. In five weeks in 1958, the Herrmanns ducked and gasped as objects flew about the room, bottles blew their tops and sailed through the air, and furniture moved itself. At one point a heavy, 20-inch statuette hurled itself across a room, and a bookcase full of large volumes moved out from a wall to wedge itself between a radiator and a bed.

All the resources of a modern community were brought to bear on the Herrmanns' problem. Police lab experts tested the house for traces of trick gadgets and chemicals (12-year-old Jimmy Herrmann was a top science student), and found nothing incriminating. Building inspectors combed the walls and foundations for structural defects, without result. Lighting company technicians also drew a blank when they made vibration tests with delicate instruments. But a Brookhaven National Laboratories physicist pointed out that there was an underground stream beneath the Herrmann house, and a combination of hard-frozen ground and partly frozen underground water might have set up weird ultrasonic vibrations. James Herrmann himself noted that almost all the poltergeist pranks took place along one geographic axis, the direction of the underground stream. But if the stream was to blame, why did the disturbances cease after five weeks?

There were no underground streams to account for the troubles that Mr. Elwin Wilson had with the house he bought in Camden, South Carolina, in 1950. At first the fun was all outside. Whenever Wilson worked in his yard, dust would spurt up around him in little puffs, almost as if someone were throwing pebbles at him. But there were no pebbles.

After the Wilson poltergeist moved inside the house, Wilson and his wife were forced to move out. "We could have put up with the footsteps tramping back and forth upstairs all night, and the banging on the walls," said Wilson. "But the thing that finished me was the invisible anvil. I was bone tired one afternoon, and lay down to rest. All of a sudden — *Whump!* Down comes something right beside me on the bed. I couldn't see it, but I could see the deep dent it made in the mattress, just the size and shape of an anvil! It hit with such force it broke the slats in the bed. I got out of the house in a hurry."

Who can blame him? Certainly not Detective Sergeant Joseph Tozzi, of the Nassau County Police in Long Island, New York.

Sergeant Tozzi was in charge of the police investigation of the James Herrmann poltergeist case. "I've never forgotten the Herrmann case, and anyone who goes through such an experience has my sympathy," he said. "There's never been any explanation of what caused those things to happen in Seaford. All I know for sure is that no one in the Herrmann family had anything to do with it. Not that I believe in poltergeists, you understand. But frankly, I think it will be a mystery forever."

THE GREAT AMHERST MYSTERY

by Walter Hubbell

Condensed and adapted

Amherst, Nova Scotia, is a beautiful vil-lage, situated on the famous Bay of Fundy. It has a population of about three thousand five hundreds souls, and contains four churches, an Academy, and a Music Hall where plays and operas are frequently given. It also has a large iron foundry, a large shoe factory, and probably more stores of various kinds than any other village of its size in the province.

In this little village there was on Princess Street a neat two-story cottage painted yellow. It was the home of Daniel Teed, a shoemaker whom everybody knew and respected.

Daniel's family consisted of his wife, Olive, his son Willie, aged five years, and his son George, aged seventeen months. Daniel also had under his roof and protection his wife's two sisters, Jennie and Esther Cox. Jennie was a self-possessed young woman of about twenty-two and quite a beauty. Esther, who was about nineteen, was short and inclined to be stout.

There were two other boarders in the cottage, also: John Teed, Daniel's brother, and William Cox, his brother-in-law.

The family of Daniel Teed rarely required the services of a physician, but when any member of the household was ill, Dr. Carritte was always called. Dr. Carritte is a gentleman of culture and refinement, and of very high standing in his profession. Almost from the first, he knew about and observed the frightful calamity that suddenly descended on the Teed family. More than once he has corroborated my statements on this subject, and I know he will be happy to do so again in the future. For I am fully aware that there are thousands of people who will not believe a word I have written, and to them I now say that, if they will consult the files of the Amherst *Gazette*, from August 28, 1878, to August 1, 1879, or call upon any of the persons whose names appear in this narrative, they will find that all my statements are just what I claim them to be

— simply, the truth, which is legally sworn in my affidavit.

It began one night at about 9 p.m. The family were all in bed in the four small bedrooms on the second story. The room in which Jennie and Esther slept was in the front of the house at the head of the stairs, and had one window directly over the front door. The two girls had lain perfectly quiet for about ten minutes, when suddenly Esther jumped out of bed, screaming that there was a mouse under the bedclothes. Her scream woke her sister, who also got out of bed and lighted the kerosene lamp. They both searched the bed but could not find the mouse.

"It's silly of us to be afraid of a harmless little mouse," said Jennie. "See, it's inside the mattress; look how the straw is being moved about by it. It's gotten inside the mattress somehow and can't get out. Let's go back to bed; it can't hurt us now."

So they put out the light and got into bed again. After listening for a few minutes without hearing the straw move in the mattress, the girls feel asleep.

On the following night the girls heard something moving underneath the bed, and Esther exclaimed, "There's that mouse again! Let's get up and kill it. I'm not going to let a mouse bother me like this every night."

So they got up and lighted the lamp. Hearing

a rustling noise in a green cardboard box filled with patchwork which was under the bed, they put the box in the middle of the room. Immediately the box sprang up into the air about a foot, and then fell to the floor and turned over onto its side. Unable to believe their eyes, the girls again placed the box upright in the middle of the room. But, even as they both watched it intently, the box repeated the same performance.

Jennie and Esther were now thoroughly frightened, and they began to scream for Daniel. Hurriedly, that gentleman put on some clothing and ran into their room to see what was the matter. But when they described what had happened, he only laughed, and after pushing the box back under the bed, remarked that they had either gone crazy or been dreaming. Then, grumbling, he went back to bed.

The next night after supper Esther complained of feeling feverish, and was advised by Mrs. Teed and Jennie to go to bed, which she did. At about ten o'clock Jennie also retired. After she had been in bed with Esther some fifteen minutes, the latter jumped with a sudden bound into the center of the room, taking all the bedclothes with her.

"My God! What's the matter with me?" she cried. "I'm dying!"

On jumping out of bed and lighting the lamp, Jennie saw an alarming sight. Esther's short hair was almost standing on end, her face was blood-red, and her eyes looked as if they were about to leap from their sockets. Jennie yelled for help, and Mrs. Teed, Daniel, William Cox, and John Teed all came on the run.

"What in thunder ails you, Esther?" demanded Daniel, while William and John exclaimed in the same breath, "She's mad!"

Suddenly Esther turned pale and became so weak that she had to be helped back to the bed. After sitting on the edge of the bed for a moment, gazing around the room with a vacant stare, she jumped to her feet again with a wild yell. "I'm swelling up, I'm going to burst, I know I am!" she cried.

"Why, she is swelling," said Daniel in a startled voice. "Olive, just look at her. Even her hands are swollen. Touch her; she's as hot as fire!"

With her entire body now blown up like a balloon, Esther was screaming with pain and grinding her teeth as if in an epileptic fit. Then suddenly there was a loud report that sounded like a clap of thunder, except that there was no rumbling afterward.

Mrs. Teed cried, "My God! The house has been struck by lightning and my boys have been killed." She rushed from the room, followed by all three men; but when they reached the children they found both sleeping peacefully.

Then all went back to the girls' room and stood looking at Esther in silence. Going to the window, Mrs. Teed raised the curtain and looked out. The stars were shining brightly, so the noise could not have been thunder. But just as she let the curtain down again, three terrific reports were heard in the room, apparently coming from under the bed on which Esther now lay. Esther, who a moment before had been so swollen, immediately resumed her natural appearance and dropped off to sleep.

About four nights later, Esther had another attack. It came on at ten o'clock, just as she was getting into bed. Jennie told her to lie perfectly still in the hope that it would go away, and Esther did so for about five minutes. Then suddenly all the bedclothes, except the bottom sheet, on which they were lying, flew off and settled down in a heap in a far corner of the room. The girls could see them passing through the air by the light of the lamp, which was still burning. Both screamed at the top of their lungs, and Jennie fainted.

Again the entire family rushed into the girls' room. There lay all the bedclothes in the corner; Esther was fearfully swollen and Jennie was lying as if dead.

Mrs. Teed snatched up the bedclothes and covered the girls with them. But she had no sooner done this than the bedclothes flew off again to the same corner of the room, and

Esther's pillow came out from under her head, flew through the air, and struck John Teed in the face.

"I've had enough of this," said he, and left the room. Nor could he be persuaded to come back and help the others hold the bedclothes down by sitting on the edge of the bed.

By this time Jennie had regained consciousness, and William Cox went down to the kitchen for a bucket of water to bathe Esther's head, which was aching. Just as he returned with the water, there was a succession of loud reports that seemed to come from the bed. They were so loud that the whole room trembled from the vibrations. Esther, who a moment before had been swollen, resumed her natural appearance and went to sleep.

At breakfast the next morning the family all agreed that a doctor had better be sent for. So in the afternoon Daniel left the shoe factory early and went to see Dr. Carritte. The doctor laughed heartily when Daniel told him what had happened, but he said he would call in the evening and remain until the next morning if necessary. He added that what Daniel had told him was all nonsense, and that he was certain no such tomfoolery would occur while he was in the house.

Esther had been in bed for an hour by the time Dr. Carritte arrived that night, and everything appeared to be normal. The doctor felt her pulse, looked at her tongue, and announced that she seemed to be suffering from nervous excitement. She had evidently received a tremendous shock of some kind, he said. Just after he had given this opinion, and while he was still sitting by her side, her pillow came out from under her head, except for one corner, as if it were being pulled by some invisible power. Then it straightened itself out, as if filled with air, hovered a moment, and went back under her head again.

The doctor's large blue eyes opened wide and he said, "Did you see that? It went back again."

"So it did," said John Teed, "but if it comes out again it won't go back, because I'll hold on to it."

He had no sooner spoken than out came the pillow from under Esther's head as before. John waited until it started back again and then grasped it with both hands. But no matter how hard he pulled, it seemed that a strength greater than his was pulling it in the opposite direction, and soon the pillow was back in place, under Esther's head.

"Amazing!" exclaimed Dr. Carritte. He rose from his chair, and just then the loud thunderclaps began to sound from under the bed. The doctor looked under there but could see nothing that might cause them. He walked to the door and the thunderclaps followed him, now seeming to come from the floor. A minute later the bedclothes flew off again, and before they could be gathered and put back, the distinct sound of a metallic instrument scraping across the wall was heard. They all looked at the wall and, to their astonishment, saw that something had been written there: "Esther Cox, you are mine to kill."

I have seen this writing. It was deeply indented in the wall and looked to me as if it had been written with a dull instrument such as a large iron spike. The letters, which were nearly a foot high, had a very uneven appearance. Obviously, the invisible power that wrote them was neither an elegant nor an accomplished penman.

As Dr. Carritte stood in the doorway wondering what it all meant, a large piece of plaster came flying from the wall of the room, turning a corner in its flight, and fell at his feet. The good doctor picked it up mechanically and placed it on a chair; he was too astonished to speak. Just then the loud pounding sounds started again with redoubled fury, this time shaking the entire room and the people in it.

The phenomena continued for about two hours, and then stopped.

When Dr. Carritte called the next morning, he was surprised to see Esther up and dressed, helping Mrs. Teed wash the breakfast dishes.

She told him she felt all right again, except that she was so nervous any sudden noise made her jump.

Having occasion to go down into the cellar with a pan of milk, she came running up, out of breath, and said there was someone in the cellar that had thrown a piece of plank at her. The doctor went down to see for himself, Esther remaining in the dining room (the cellar door opened into the dining room). In a moment Dr. Carritte came up again and assured her there was no one down there to throw a piece of plank or anything else.

"Come down with me, Esther," he said.

As they were going down together, several potatoes came flying at their heads, and they ran back up the stairs rather hastily.

The doctor then left the house, but called again in the evening with several very powerful sedatives, which he administered to Esther at about ten o'clock, as she lay in bed. She still complained of nervousness, and said she felt as if electricity were shooting all through her body. Dr. Carritte had just given her the medicine and told her that she would have a good night's sleep when the noises started again, only this time they came in more rapid succession than before. Presently the sounds left the room and moved to the roof of the house. The doctor went outside and into the street, where he heard the noises in the open air. He said afterwards that it sounded as if someone were on the roof with a heavy sledge-hammer, pounding the shingles. Yet, since it was a moonlit night, he could see distinctly that there was no one on the roof.

About one month after the haunting started, the Reverend Dr. Edwin Clay, a Baptist clergy-man, called at the house to see and hear the wonders of which he had read some accounts in the newspapers. While he was there the sounds were at their loudest; he also saw the writing on the wall. When he left, he was fully satisfied that Esther was not producing the noises herself, and that the family had nothing what-ever to do with them. He agreed with Dr. Carritte that Esther's nerves must have received a shock of some kind, and he developed the theory that, in some mysterious manner, this shock had turned her into a kind of electric battery. Mr. Clay's idea was that invisible flashes of lightning came from Esther's body and that the sounds were simply tiny peals of thunder. So convinced was he that he had dis-covered the cause that he delivered lectures on the subject and drew large audiences.

The Reverend R. A. Temple, pastor of the Methodist Church in Amherst, which the Teed family attended, also witnessed the manifesta-tions. He saw, among other strange things, a bucket of cold water apparently come to a boil while standing on the kitchen table.

The disturbances continued until December, when Esther was taken ill with diphtheria and confined to her bed for about two weeks. During this period the power ceased to torment her.

Not long after her recovery, however, the phenomena resumed in a new and more dangerous form. One night Esther told Jennie that she could hear a voice informing her that the house was about to be set on fire by a ghost. The voice said it had once lived on the earth, but had been dead for some years and was now only a spirit.

The girls at once called in the other members of the household, and gave them the ghost's message. But the others just laughed. There were no ghosts there, they insisted. After all, the Reverend Dr. Clay had explained that the trouble was caused by electricity.

While they were laughing at the ridiculous idea of a ghost setting fire to the house, a lighted match fell from the ceiling to the bed. It would have set fire to the bedding if Jennie hadn't put it out instantly. During the next ten minutes eight or ten lighted matches fell out of the air, but all were extinguished before they could do any damage. There was no more laughter, of course — just a fearful question addressed to the invisible power, and a frightening answer.

It seems that about three weeks after Dr.

Carritte's first visit to the cottage, he and the family had worked out a system of communicating with the power by means of a rapping code. They would ask it questions and it would knock once for "no," three times for "yes," or twice for "not sure." So it was in this way that they carried on a conversation the night the matches fell from the ceiling.

Daniel asked if the house would really be set on fire. The reply was yes. And within five minutes a fire was started, in the following manner. The ghost took a dress belonging to Esther that was hanging on a nail in the wall and, after rolling it up and placing it under the bed before their eyes — but so fast that they could not prevent the action — set it on fire. Fortunately, Daniel was able to pull it out from under the bed quickly and put out the flames.

After that, all was quiet for the rest of the night, but no one dared to go to bed, for fear another fire would be kindled.

A few days later Mrs. Teed, while churning butter in the kitchen, noticed smoke issuing from the cellar door. Esther was seated in the dining room and had been there for an hour or more, previous to which she had been in the kitchen helping her sister.

Mrs. Teed seized a bucket of drinking water and rushed down the cellar stairs. In the far corner of the cellar she saw a pile of wood shavings blazing up almost to the main floor of the house. After pouring the water over the shavings, Mrs. Teed, accompanied by Esther, ran out of the house into Princess Street, both shouting, "Fire, fire!" as loudly as they could.

Their cries aroused the entire neighborhood. Several men rushed in and smothered the fire with rugs from the dining-room floor.

The Amherst *Gazette* published an account of the fire, and as the article was copied throughout Canada, a tremendous sensation was created. Thousands of people who had set the whole affair down as a first-class fraud began to think there might be something in it after all; for certainly no girl could set fire to a pile of shavings in the cellar and be at the same time in one of the rooms above, under the watchful eye of an elder sister. The fact that both the little Teed boys were playing in the front yard at the time freed them of suspicion, too.

The firemen of Amherst thought Esther must have started the fire in some unexplained manner. Other people had various theories. Dr. Nathan Tupper, who had never witnessed a single manifestation, suggested that if a strong rawhide whip was laid across Esther's bare shoulders by a powerful arm, the tricks of the girl would cease at once.

Only the family and Dr. Carritte knew that the fire had been started by the ghost.

Postscript: Most poltergeist stories don't come to a neatly wrapped-up conclusion — they just stop, usually as unexpectedly as they began. The power, or whatever it is that causes the phenomena, peters out after a few weeks or months. Esther Cox's story is no exception. Eventually she got married and had a child. When in 1907 author Hereward Carrington came to check on Hubbell's report, the most important witness, Dr. Carritte, had long since died. However, he did talk with Mrs. Teed, who said that Hubbell's account was generally accurate, although he had dressed it up a little to make it more exciting. Carrington also visited Esther, whom he described as sullen and evidently not very contented in her marriage. At first she told him she couldn't remember what had happened, but later she suggested that her memory might improve if he gave her $100. Knowing that paid testimony is almost never worth the price, Carrington left without visiting her again.

—M.B.

SCIENCE GOES TO A SÉANCE

*"I never said it was possible;
I only said it was true."*

— Sir William Crookes

When William Crookes announced that he was going to test some self-proclaimed psychic mediums under laboratory conditions, his fellow scientists all over Britain applauded him. "Now at last," they said, "these people who claim to talk with spirits of the dead, levitate tables, and other such nonsense will be exposed as the fakers they are. Whatever William Crookes says will be accepted without question by scientists and laymen alike."

But when Crookes made his first report on the medium Daniel Dunglas Home (pronounced "Hume"), it was not accepted. Instead, it aroused a storm of ridicule that threatened to destroy his reputation as one of the most brilliant young scientists in Britain. He was attacked by newspaper editors, denounced by clergymen, and scolded by his colleagues in the Royal Society (a most exclusive "club" of scientists, founded in 1660).

What displeased his critics so much was that Crookes had not exposed Home as a fraud but instead had pronounced him an honest man. He had tested the medium in his own laboratory, where he could take every precaution against trickery and keep Home under close scrutiny all the time. And even under the most stringent test conditions, Home was able to make a wooden board get heavier without touching it; call forth a disembodied finger and thumb which plucked petals from a flower in his buttonhole and laid them in front of several people who were sitting near him; cause an accordion to hover in the air and play itself; and perform many other impossible-sounding feats. Crookes agreed with his critics that such things were contrary to everything that rational people had been taught to believe. Yet, he was convinced that Home had not cheated, and he felt it was his duty as a seeker after truth to publish what he had seen with his own eyes.

In 1871 Crookes heard of another medium, a girl of fifteen named Florence Cook. Not long before, Florence had attended a spectacular séance, and the experience had inspired her to try to develop her own mediumistic powers. Soon she was giving séances at which the phantom form of a woman materialized out of nowhere while Florence was in a trance. The phantom was amazingly lifelike as she walked around the room and chatted with the sitters. She gave her name as Katie King. She said she had been the daughter of John King, had lived in India, had been married, and had murdered her two children.

Crookes tested Florence Cook at intervals for three years, until she was eighteen. His articles about the Katie King phenomenon drew an even greater torrent of abuse than he had endured before. He was accused of collaborating with Miss Cook to hoodwink the public, and of carrying on a secret love affair with her. Even today, more than a hundred years later, the debate has not died out completely.

William Crookes became "Sir" William in 1897 when he was knighted by Queen Victoria. Of course the honor was given in recognition of such important scientific achievements as his discovery of the element thallium and his invention of the radiometer. Katie King was not mentioned.

—M.B.

THE SPIRIT-FORM OF KATIE KING

by Sir William Crookes

Condensed and adapted

Last February, speaking of the phenomena of spirit-forms which have appeared through Miss Florence Cook's mediumship, I said, "Let those who are inclined to judge Miss Cook harshly suspend their judgment until I bring forward positive evidence which I think will settle the question. Miss Cook is now devoting herself exclusively to a series of private séances with me and one or two friends. Enough has taken place to thoroughly convince me of the perfect truth and honesty of Miss Cook." I am happy to say that I have at last obtained the "absolute proof" to which I referred.

I will pass over most of the tests which Katie King (the spirit-form that appeared while Miss

Cook was in trance) has given me and will only describe one or two recent tests. For some time I have been experimenting with a phosphorus lamp consisting of a tightly corked six- or eight-ounce bottle containing a little phosphorized oil. I hoped that by the light of this lamp some of the mysterious phenomena of the cabinet might be made visible.

On March 12th, during a séance, after Katie had been walking amongst us and talking for some time, she retreated behind the curtain which separated my laboratory, where the company were sitting, from my library, which served as a cabinet. In a minute she came to the curtain and called me to her, saying, "Come into the room and lift my medium's head up, she has slipped down." Katie was then standing before me clothed in her usual white robes and turban headdress. I walked into the library and up to Miss Cook, Katie stepping aside to allow me to pass. I found that Miss Cook had slipped partially off the sofa, and her head was hanging in a very awkward position. I lifted her onto the sofa, and in so doing had satisfactory evidence, in spite of the darkness, that Miss Cook was not attired in the "Katie" costume, but had on her ordinary black velvet dress, and was in a deep trance. Not more than three seconds elapsed between my seeing the white-robed Katie standing before me and my raising Miss Cook onto the sofa.

After I returned to my observation post by the curtain, Katie again appeared and said she thought she would be able to show herself and her medium to me at the same time. The gas was then turned out, and she asked for my phosphorus lamp. After exhibiting herself by it for some seconds, she handed it back to me, saying, "Now come in and see my medium." I closely followed her into the library, and by the light of my lamp saw Miss Cook lying on the sofa just as I had left her. I looked around for Katie, but she had disappeared. I called her, but there was no answer.

I resumed my place. Katie soon reappeared and told me that she had been standing close to Miss Cook all the time. She then asked if she might try an experiment herself, and taking the phosphorus lamp from me she passed behind the curtain, asking me not to look in just now. In a few minutes she handed the lamp back to me, saying she could not succeed, as she had used up all the power, but would try again another time. My eldest son, a boy of fourteen, who was sitting opposite me in such a position that he could see behind the curtain, tells me he distinctly saw the phosphorus lamp apparently floating about in space over Miss Cook, illuminating her as she lay motionless on the sofa, but he could not see anyone holding the lamp.

I pass on to a séance held last night at Hackney. Katie never appeared to greater perfection, and for nearly two hours she walked about the room, conversing familiarly with those present. Several times she took my arm when walking, and I had the strong impression that it was a living woman by my side, instead of a visitor from the other world. To verify this, I asked her permission to clasp her in my arms. Permission was graciously given, and I accordingly did — well, what any gentleman would do under the circumstances. The "ghost" was as material a being as Miss Cook herself.

Katie now said she thought she would be able this time to show herself and Miss Cook together. I was to turn the gas out, and then come with my phosphorus lamp into the cabinet.

I went cautiously into the room, it being dark, and felt about for Miss Cook. I found her crouching on the floor. Kneeling down, I let air enter the lamp, and by its light I saw the young lady dressed in black velvet, as she had been before, and apparently unconscious. She did not move when I took her hand and held the light quite close to her face.

Raising the lamp, I looked around and saw Katie standing close behind Miss Cook. She was robed in flowing white drapery as we had seen her previously. Holding one of Miss Cook's hands in mine, and still kneeling, I passed the lamp up and down so as to illuminate Katie's whole figure. She did not speak, but moved her head and smiled in recognition.

Three separate times did I carefully examine Miss Cook crouching before me, to be sure that the hand I held was that of a living woman, and three separate times did I turn the lamp to Katie and examine her with steadfast scrutiny, until I had no doubt whatever of her objective reality. At last Miss Cook moved slightly, and Katie instantly motioned me to go away. I went to another part of the cabinet and then ceased to see Katie, but did not leave the room till Miss Cook woke up, and two of the visitors came in with a light.

Before concluding, I wish to give some of the points of difference which I have observed between Miss Cook and Katie. Katie's height varies; in my house I have seen her six inches taller than Miss Cook. Last night, with bare feet and not "tiptoeing," she was four and a half inches taller than Miss Cook. Katie's neck was bare last night; the skin was perfectly smooth both to touch and sight, whereas Miss Cook's neck has a large blister on it which is distinctly visible and rough to the touch. Katie's ears are unpierced, while Miss Cook habitually wears earrings. Katie's complexion is very fair, while that of Miss Cook is very dark. Katie's fingers are much longer than Miss Cook's, and her face is also larger. In manners and ways of expression there are also many differences.

Katie's Last Appearance

During the week before Katie took her departure she gave séances at my house almost nightly, to enable me to photograph her by artificial light. Five cameras were focused on Katie simultaneously, on each occasion when she stood for her portrait.

My library was used as a dark cabinet. It has folding doors opening into the laboratory; one of these doors was taken off its hinges, and a curtain hung in its place to enable Katie to pass in and out easily. The friends who were present were seated in the laboratory facing the curtain, and the cameras were placed a little behind them. Each evening there were three or four exposures of plates in each of the five cameras, giving at least fifteen separate pictures at each séance. Some of these were spoiled in the developing, and some in regulating the amount of light. Altogether I have forty-four negatives, some inferior, some indifferent, and some excellent.

Katie instructed all the other sitters to keep their seats, but for some time past she has given me permission to do what I like — to touch her, and to enter and leave the cabinet almost whenever I pleased.

During the last six months Miss Cook has been a frequent visitor at my house, remaining sometimes a week at a time. She brings nothing with her but a little hand-bag, not locked; during the day she is constantly in the presence of Mrs. Crookes, myself, or some other member of my family. As she does not sleep by herself, there is absolutely no opportunity for any preparation even of a less elaborate character than would be required for enacting Katie King.

I myself prepare my library as the dark cabinet, and usually, after Miss Cook has been dining and conversing with us, and scarcely out of our sight for a minute, she walks directly into the cabinet. I lock its second door and keep possession of the key all through the séance. The gas is then turned out, and Miss Cook is left in darkness.

On entering the cabinet Miss Cook lies down on the floor with her head on a pillow, and is soon in a trance. During the photographic séances, Katie muffled her medium's head in a shawl to prevent the light from falling on her face. I frequently drew the curtain on one side when Katie was standing near, and it was a common thing for the seven or eight of us in the laboratory to see Miss Cook and Katie

105

at the same time, under the full blaze of the electric light. We did not actually see the medium's face because of the shawl, but we saw her hands and feet; we saw her move uneasily under the intense light, and we heard her moan occasionally. I have one photograph of the two together, but Katie is seated in front of Miss Cook's head.

One of the most interesting of the pictures is one in which I am standing by the side of Katie; she has her bare foot upon a particular part of the floor. Afterwards I dressed Miss Cook like Katie, placed her and myself in exactly the same position, and we were photographed by the same cameras, placed exactly as in the other experiment, and illuminated by the same light. When these two pictures are placed over each other, the two photographs of me coincide exactly as regards height, etc., but Katie is half a head taller than Miss Cook and looks like a big woman in comparison with her.

Having seen Katie so much lately under the electric light, I am able to add to the points of difference between her and her medium which I mentioned earlier. Several little marks on Miss Cook's face are absent on Katie's. Miss Cook's hair is so dark a brown as almost to appear black; a lock of Katie's which is now before me and which she allowed me to cut off, having first traced it up to the scalp and satisfied myself that it actually grew there, is a rich golden auburn.

One evening I timed Katie's pulse. It beat steadily at 75, whereas Miss Cook's pulse a little later was going at its usual rate of 90. On applying my ear to Katie's chest I could hear a heart beating rhythmically inside. Tested in the same way, Katie's lungs were found to be sounder than her medium's, for at the time Miss Cook was under treatment for a severe cough.

When the time came for Katie to take her farewell, I asked that she let me see the last of her. Accordingly, when she had called each of the company up to her and had spoken to them a few words in private, she gave some general directions for the future guidance and protection of Miss Cook. Then Katie invited me into the cabinet with her.

After closing the curtain she conversed with me for some time, and then walked across the room to where Miss Cook was lying unconscious on the floor. Stooping over her, Katie touched her and said, "Wake up, Florrie, wake up! I must leave you now."

Miss Cook then woke and tearfully begged Katie to stay a while longer.

"My dear, I can't; my work is done. God bless you," Katie replied.

Then for several minutes the two conversed with each other, till at last Miss Cook's tears prevented her from speaking. Following Katie's instructions, I then came forward to support Miss Cook, who was sobbing hysterically. I looked round, but the white-robed Katie had gone.

As soon as Miss Cook was sufficiently calmed, a light was brought and I led her out of the cabinet.

WHAT IF . . . ?

What if you slept? And what if, in your
sleep, you dreamed? And what if,
in your dream, you went to heaven and
there plucked a strange and beautiful
flower? And what if, when you awoke,
you had the flower in your hand?
Ah, what then?

— *Samuel Taylor Coleridge*

None of the people in the following three
stories went to heaven during sleep and woke
up with flowers in their hands to prove it.
But all of them did go to some far-off place
during sleep, and all woke up with new information in their heads that might help
prove it.

While their bodies lay asleep in bed, it seemed to them that their consciousnesses put on another kind of body and went traveling. They visited places where they had never been before, and saw people they had never met. After a while they returned and "got back into" their physical bodies. Later they found out that the places and people they had seen really existed, and looked exactly as they had envisioned them.

Can we explain away such an experience by calling it "an unusually vivid dream"? Not if the information that the person picked up was accurate and could not possibly have reached him by normal means.

Then how about calling it "an unusually vivid *clairvoyant* dream"? That would seem to dispose of the mystery — except for one more factor, which may be the most puzzling of all:

In each of the three cases you are about to read, the person was actually seen by one or more wide-awake people in the place he "traveled" to!

—M.B.

THE DREAM HOUSE

Anonymous

This case was told to a magazine editor by a man who asked that his name not be revealed.

Some time ago, my wife dreamed on several occasions of a house whose interior arrangement she was able to describe in all its details, although she had no idea where this house was.

Later, in 1883, I leased from Lady B—, for the autumn, a house in the mountains of Scotland, surrounded by hunting lands and fishing lakes. My son, who was then in Scotland, took charge of the matter, without my wife or I ever seeing the house in question.

When I went there alone later, to sign the contract and take possession of the property, Lady B— was still living in the house. She told me that if I had no objection she would give me a room which she herself had been occupying and which had, for some time, been haunted by a woman who continued to appear there.

Being quite skeptical about such matters, I replied that I should be delighted to make the acquaintance of the ghost. I went to sleep in the room, but did not see any ghost.

Later, when my wife arrived, she was astonished when she recognized the house as the one of her dreams! She went all over it; all the details corresponded with those she had so often seen in sleep. But when she went into the drawing room again, she said: "But still, this cannot be the house I saw in my dreams, because there ought to be a succession of rooms that are missing here." She was told that the rooms actually existed, but that one could not reach them through the drawing-room. When they were shown to her, she remembered each one of them clearly.

She said, however, that it seemed to her that one of the bedrooms was not used for this purpose when she visited it in her dreams. It was explained to her that this room had not formerly been a bedroom, but had been changed into one.

Two or three days later my wife and I visited Lady B—. Since they were unknown to each other, I introduced them. Lady B— cried out in amazement: "Why — you are the lady who has been haunting my bedroom!"

A VISITOR AT SEA

by Mr. Wilmot

This case of astral projection or out-of-body experience (OOBE) is unusual in that it is supported by the testimony of three persons: the projector herself, and two witnesses. One witness was asleep and dreaming, or thought he was; but the other was wide awake. The case was told to psychic researchers by one of the witnesses, Mr. Wilmot.

On October 3rd, 1863, I sailed from Liverpool, England, for New York, on the steamer *City of Limerick*, of the Inman line, Captain Jones commanding. On the evening of our second day out a severe storm began, which lasted for nine days. During this time we saw neither sun nor stars nor any other vessel. One of the anchors broke loose from its lashings and did considerable damage before it could be secured, several stout storm sails were carried away, and the booms broken.

On the night following the eighth day of the storm the wind moderated a little, and for the first time since leaving port I enjoyed refreshing sleep. Toward morning I dreamed that I saw my wife, whom I had left at home in the United States, come to the door of my stateroom, dressed in her nightgown. At the door she seemed to discover that I was not the only occupant of the room, hesitated a little, then advanced to my side. She stooped down and kissed me, and after gently caressing me for a few moments, quietly withdrew.

Upon waking I was surprised to see my roommate, whose berth was above mine — but not directly over it, owing to the fact that our room was at the stern of the vessel — leaning upon his elbow and looking fixedly at me. "You're a pretty fellow," said he at length, "to have a lady come and visit you in this way!"

I pressed him for an explanation, which he at first declined to give, but at length he related what he had seen while wide awake, lying in his berth. It exactly corresponded with my dream.

This gentleman's name was William J. Tait. A native of England, and the son of a clergyman of the Church of England, he had for a number of years lived in Cleveland, Ohio, where he held the position of librarian of the Associated Library. He was at this time perhaps fifty years of age, by no means in the habit of practical joking, but a sedate and very religious man, whose testimony upon any subject could be taken unhesitatingly.

The day after landing I went by rail to Watertown, Connecticut, where my children and my wife had been for some time, visiting her parents. Almost her first question when we were alone together was "Did you receive a visit from me a week ago Tuesday?"

"A visit from you?" said I. "We were more than a thousand miles at sea."

"I know it," she replied, "but it seemed to me that I visited you."

"It would be impossible," said I. "Tell me what makes you think so."

My wife then told me that on account of the severity of the weather and the reported loss of the *Africa* (which had sailed for Boston on the same day that we left Liverpool for New York, and had gone ashore at Cape Race), she had been extremely anxious about me. On the same night when, as mentioned above, the storm had just begun to abate, she had lain awake for a long time thinking of me, and

116

about four o'clock in the morning it seemed to her that she went out to seek me.

Crossing the wide and stormy sea, she came at length to a low, black steamship, whose side she went up, and then descending into the cabin, passed through it to the stern until she came to my stateroom. "Tell me," said she, "do they ever have staterooms like the one I saw, where the upper berth extends further back than the lower one? A man was in the upper berth, looking right at me, and for a moment I was afraid to go in. But soon I went up to the side of your berth, bent down and kissed you, and embraced you, and then went away."

The description given by my wife of the steamship was correct in all particulars, though she had never seen it!

A NOTE ABOUT
"THE TWENTY-FIFTH MAN"

Sometime in the late 1890's a group of convicts were transferred from Folsom Prison, in California, to San Quentin Prison. Ed. Morrell, No. 16,766, was the 25th man of the Folsom transfer.

Strictly speaking, Morrell was not a criminal; he was a California feud outlaw, which was something different.

The California feud was fought between settlers of the San Joaquin Valley and the railroad that owned their land. The railroad corporation, which had been granted large tracts of land along the right-of-way by the federal government, decided to offer homesteads at $5 an acre to any who would live

118

on and improve the land for a certain number of years. Hundreds accepted the offer and moved in to build houses, dig wells, and plant crops. But when the trial period was up, the railroad announced that since the land had been improved it was now worth $27 to $60 an acre. Because most of the settlers were unable to pay the higher prices, they were forced to leave their homes, with nothing to show for their years of hard work.

After their expulsion, some of these embittered homesteaders banded together to wage a kind of guerrilla warfare against the railroad. Their chief tactic was to stop trains and take money from the express cars; they never robbed the passengers.

Ed. Morrell was not one of the dispossessed settlers, but he sympathized with their cause so strongly that he joined the outlaw band. The exploit that led to his arrest was his holdup of the Fresno County Jail and the release of an outlaw prisoner. As the two were fleeing from the jail, they were confronted by the Chief of Police. Morrell took the Chief's gun away from him to prevent him from shooting as they dashed off in a horse-drawn wagon. Later, trapped in a farmhouse surrounded by a sheriff's posse, Morrell gave himself up without firing a shot.

He expected to be tried for the county

jail holdup, which carried a maximum penalty of ten years. Instead, he was tried for the theft of a law officer's gun, a much more serious crime. His case was heard by twelve professional jurymen whose salaries were paid by the railroad. The verdict was guilty; the sentence: life imprisonment.

In Folsom Prison, Morrell took part in a strike protesting inhuman conditions in the jute mill where many of the convicts were made to work. This earned him a reputation as a troublemaker, and meant that he was under suspicion from the first day he entered San Quentin. Thus, when another convict told the warden that Morrell was planning a mutiny and had weapons hidden somewhere in the prison, the warden readily believed the story.

Morrell was tried by prison officials on these new trumped-up charges, found guilty, and sentenced to solitary confinement for the rest of his natural life. His stubborn insistence that he was innocent only enraged the warden further. Maybe if he tortured Morrell, the warden decided, he could make him tell where the weapons were hidden. The instrument of torture that he chose was a canvas straitjacket, or, to give a more accurate impression of its size, a straitcoat. The victim was to be laced into this coat as tightly as his brawny guards could manage.

The following excerpts from Morrell's autobiography begin the story just after his first siege in the straitjacket: four days and fourteen hours of agonizing constriction.

—M.B.

THE TWENTY-FIFTH MAN

by Ed. Morrell

Condensed and adapted

They cut the ropes and rolled me out. What
a sight I beheld! My hands, arms, and legs
were frightfully bruised. My body was shriveled
like that of an old man, and a horrible stench
came from it.

Crawling to the water bucket, I bathed the
stinging bruises and washed off the smearings
of hardened blood where the ropes had cut
into the flesh. And then, entirely exhausted, I
sank down upon my mattress, covered myself
with a blanket, and did not arise from it for
a week.

During that week all the horrors of my life
trooped through my dazed mind. I had been
roughly transplanted from a free and easy

environment to a prison hell, to suffer the most fiendish tortures and finally to be confined in a solitary dungeon for the balance of my natural life. And that was not all. Here I must endure the bloody straightjacket. Until now I had always felt there was a way out, but the straitjacket had reduced me to despair.

I slept a strange sleep. I seemed to be awake and yet I was dreaming. I was conscious of the nearness of friends, a host of them, and yet no living being could enter that dungeon except my enemies.

Suddenly I felt myself being led. Voices commanded me and I obeyed. I performed many daring feats and went through unimaginable tests of bravery. It was like going through the rites of a weird initiation.

At last came the most terrible ordeal of all. I stepped into a punishment room. Big Bill Smith, my detective employer, was there; gunmen who had hunted me for my head price were there. The Folsom warden, the San Quentin warden, prison rats and stool pigeons and in fact everybody who had harmed me was there. All of them were being tortured, racked by the same punishments that they had inflicted on me.

Before I went to sleep I had been seething with hatred for every one of them, cursing them, vowing vengeance. But now I looked at them with deep compassion; I was pained when I gazed upon their sufferings. Then came the strangest reaction of all: I went to work releasing them! I tore madly at the fetters that bound them in their misery, and did not stop for breath until I had freed all of them.

Then a new marvel occurred. A tingling sensation spread through my body and I heard a voice. It seemed to speak plainly, almost in my ear. "You have learned the unreality of pain and hence of fear.

"You have learned the futility of trying to fight your enemies with hatred," the voice went on. "You have seen that the sword of hatred is double-edged, cutting deeply into your own vitals rather than overcoming the evil which is working against you.

"From today a new life vista will open up, and you will fight from a far superior vantage point. Your weapon will be the sword of love, and as your power unfolds, this new weapon will cut away all evil forces which now oppose you. And to prove this power, even the strait-jacket will have no terrors for you. It will only be a means to greater things.

"Your life from now on must be a work of preparation, and when the time is ripe for your deliverance you will know it. The proof will be a power to prophesy to your enemies, not only the day of your release from this dungeon but also from the prison, when the great governor of the state will come in person to San Quentin and bring your pardon. Peace and love are yours!"

Slowly I opened my eyes. I was in the dungeon, but it was no longer a place of horror to me. I was a new being. My poor shrunken hands did not tremble, and the spasmodic twitching of my mouth and eyes had ceased. It seemed as if the strength of a million men was concentrated within my frame. Truly I was a new man.

This was the beginning of a series of wonderful revelations. I now realized that my mind and body were entirely separate. The proof of this came with the most appalling torture of all I had endured.

One day the Warden came down to solitary with fire in his eye. Though nearly always cool and calculating, this time he hurled oaths at the guard and ordered him to tie me in the straitjacket tighter than before, and even to pull the rope to the breaking point in order to get the least bit of slack out of it.

In that siege in the jacket I weathered one hundred and twenty-six continuous hours of constriction. It was the longest torture ever inflicted on a convict during the reign of the bloody straitjacket in San Quentin. Yet even in that extremity I did not heed the racking torment, because the supremacy of my mind over my body had been established. During my many sieges of torture in the jacket, nothing occurred in my cell of which I was not aware, even though I was absolutely dead to physical feeling or pain. This proves conclusively that my mind was always in control. I had become a master of self-hypnosis, or suspended animation — call it what you will.

Furthermore, I could direct my mind to leave my body entirely and roam at will. Sometimes, unbelievable as it may seem, my mind was projected outside of the dungeon and played a part in the lives of people I was later destined to meet.

Furious because he had been unable to squeeze the spirit — and a confession — out of Morrell with one straitjacket, the Warden decided to try two jackets and to leave Morrell in them for ten days. Accordingly, he and the dungeon guard first tied the convict as tightly as they could in one jacket and then put a second over it. While they were doing this, Morrell tauntingly offered the Warden a bet: If, when he was released from the double-jacketing, he could smile, the Warden must buy a package of tobacco for Morrell's companion in solitary, "the Tiger."

"I say, Morrell, you are a wooze," the Warden remarked. "I'll show you I'm a sport. If you are alive ten days from now, I will pay that wager, provided you can open your eyes and give me even the shadow of a smile, much less a real smile!"

Then the Warden and the guard stamped out of the cell and the door slammed to with a bang.

I was alone, and in another ten minutes the world began to sway and whirl. Would my guardian angel desert me now in this, the supreme test of all? My heart, instead of beating to seconds, was apparently stroking off one beat to the hour. The gap between beats seemed interminable.

For a moment I was afraid the conscious mind would not release its grip and let me go. I felt that I must shriek out to my tormentors and beg abjectly for mercy. But the thought of my defeat and the Warden's victory was enough. It stirred me to an unbelievable exaltation. My physical being quieted down and I no longer felt the slightest pain. My breath eased off from the steamlike rushing sensations of a moment before.

Moreover, I became convinced that the jackets were being stretched by a force outside of myself. And the uncanny part of it was that not my subconscious mind, but my physical senses clearly registered this fact. The jackets which encased me were abominably loose. To prove it to my ever-questioning mind, I freely moved my arms and hands in the pockets within the jacket. I even rolled around on the dungeon floor.

A moment later I was out of my jackets, bending down looking at my body. A great pity welled up in me. I felt the urge to watch over the body and keep it safe. I stooped low to listen to the regular breathing, but the Tiger was knuckle-tapping* now and I was afraid the noise would awaken me. I decided to go and tell him to stop it.

During my periods of self-induced hypnosis I had often wanted to project myself into the Tiger's cell. I wanted to see what he looked like and to note some definite thing he was doing, so that later I could offer him a real proof of my power. But I had failed utterly. A force over which I had no control invariably led me out and beyond the walls of the prison to travel through space with the speed of lightning, perhaps to some strange, distant land.

I might view seas, deserts, islands, rivers, with here and there flashes of the tropics, and then return in the space of a moment to scenes more homelike, and to people I knew.

San Francisco always held me spellbound. There I would flit in and out through highways

---

* Morrell and the Tiger talked to each other by means of an alphabetical tapping code.

and byways of the big city, sometimes stopping in Golden Gate Park to watch the throngs moving about.

Once I was present during a shipwreck just outside the Golden Gate. I heard the cries of women and children, saw them swallowed by the sea; and while I stood on the deck of the ship, one man adjusted a strange apparatus and floated safely away as the vessel sank beneath him. In later years I had that device patented as the Morrell Life Saving Suit.

That wreck was an actual occurrence, as I afterwards found out. It happened on the very day that I had left my body encased in the straitjacket in San Quentin's dungeon.

Another experience that took on significance later was my persistent dogging of the footsteps of a man in Alameda County, whom I in some way associated with my release from the dungeon.

Wherever I went, people riveted my attention. By some uncanny power I was able to look through and beyond them. I was fascinated.

Human beings automatically divided themselves into distinct groups. I found that each person possessed a different odor. If it was pleasant, fresh, good to smell, that person's face invariably wore a happy smile, and a bright, suffusing light surrounded the head. Those who emitted an obnoxious and fetid odor had faces almost obscured by dark shadows.

In my wanderings from the "Jacket Hell" of San Quentin, I always avoided places of evil, shunning people of "the dark shadow" and seeking out those in whom love abided.

There was one place that drew me with the force of a magnet. It was a quiet, restful town of fruit and flowers in the interior of California. On my first visit I found myself entering a large school. I recall that I did not want to go inside for fear of disturbing the pupils in their study. But again the force that irresistibly led me here and there in my pilgrimages would not be denied.

I ventured into one room and walked up the center aisle until I reached the teacher's desk. I paused there long enough to utter some apology for my intrusion, but the teacher was not aware of my presence.

I turned to look about over the sea of young faces. Suddenly my eyes rested on one, a girl of twelve or thirteen. A weird impulse attracted me toward her. I walked slowly down the aisle and stopped near her desk, which was by an open window. She raised her head as if to look at me.

When I entered the classroom I noticed that a few of the young faces were cloudy, almost in shadow. But that of the little girl I picked out was fairly radiant with light. Her blue eyes were frank, open, and trusting.

In a vague, instinctive way, I knew we were not strangers. Still, she seemed startled at my sudden appearance. I hurried to say a few reassuring words. She moved over in her seat. It seemed to be an invitation to sit down.

The afternoon session closed and the pupils filed out. My little girl carefully put her books away and was about the last to leave. I went with her. Outside another girl joined her. After a few words they parted, and we two so strangely brought together walked toward her home. She stood at the gate for a moment, pensive and, as I thought, looking into my eyes. Then she turned and entered the house.

And now at last I was in the Tiger's cell. He had quit knuckle-rapping and was lying on his back on his old straw tick.

I stood inside the cell, but near the door. My first impression was of horror. There on the sodden mattress lay the wreck of what had been a man, a mere sack of bones, reminding one of a shriveled corpse burnt black from the desert sun.

His hair was matted and he had a shaggy beard. I could see his eyes shining like two black coals. But the face! It was in shadow, and the odor from his body was overpowering.

The tragedy of the Tiger's life was now

plain. Burning hate had cluttered up the channels to his higher self. I wanted so much to help him, but a yawning chasm lay between us. I made a superhuman effort to touch him, but could not. My feet would not move and my hand refused to obey the command of my will.

The Tiger was muttering something. I heard my name and the word "jacket," and the remark "They will kill him, sure. He can't stand it. The double jacket will fix him." Then came a string of curses on the Warden's head.

I wanted to go, but the Tiger's next move riveted me to the spot, all attention. With the thumb and forefinger of his left hand he was mechanically wiggling a loose tooth in the front of his mouth, and I stood there speculating how much longer he would continue the grim operation before he jerked it out.

In another moment the Tiger's hell hole had faded, and I was back in my own cell.

The Warden, the prison doctor, and the dungeon guard had returned. It was only the fourth day after my double-jacketing; but a Senate investigating committee had come to the prison, and, fearing that the truth might leak out if I should die, the Warden ordered the guard to cut the ropes quickly. Before he did it, the prison "croaker" gave me a hasty examination.

With a leer on his face, he straightened up and coolly remarked to the Warden, "Well, you fixed him all right this time! He's as dead as a door nail."

I recall the whole thing vividly. I was standing over to one side of the cell looking down on my poor scarred body, which lay in a lifeless heap before me. I wondered if I would ever again occupy the miserable shell. It had always seemed to me that if I remained away after they took my body from the straitjacket, I wouldn't be able to get back into it again.

The guard cut the ropes and rolled me out. I was resting on my back. There was a struggle. My eyelids fluttered, opened, and in an instant I was smiling up into the Warden's face, to his great relief.

"There! There!" he shouted at the top of his voice to the croaker. "I knew he was only faking!"

"No wonder he can smile!" said the guard laconically. "He's paralyzed."

"Paralyzed!" the Warden jeered. "Get him on his feet and he'll stand all right!"

Obeying orders, the guard dragged me up, then let go. Of course after such a lacing the life could not return to my body all at once.

I reeled, bent at the knees and pitched sideways, gashing my forehead against the wall, to the great amusement of those who had tried to kill me.

"He's a fine actor. He's got nerve enough to do anything."

I replied in a husky whisper, "You're right! Of course I did that on purpose, just to amuse you. I am only sorry I couldn't have died long ago in the jacket, to put you out of the misery of having to bother torturing me.

"But," I added, "since you didn't succeed in killing me and since I smiled, I have won a little wager which will cost you just five cents. Don't forget the Tiger's sack of tobacco."

At this the Warden raised his hands to his hair as if to tear it out by the roots. Then, realizing that it was dangerous for him to remain, since he had done his worst and could do nothing now but trample me with his feet, he moved to the cell door.

My husky voice stopped him. "Just one moment, Warden. I have a little prophecy to make." And I smiled again, while the blood from the gash in my forehead trickled warmly down my face. "This is the last time I will ever be tortured in the jacket. One year from today I will go out of this dungeon never to return to it. And better still, four years from the day I leave the dungeon I will walk from the prison a free man with a pardon in my hand. What's more, the governor of the state will bring that pardon in person to San Quentin!"

Glaring with rage, the Warden cursed and stamped his feet, then dashed from the dungeon like a madman. He who had seen so many men weaken and collapse after just a few hours in that instrument of torture had given me up as one who could not be killed. They never again put me in the jacket, and my wanderings were at an end.

One day, exactly a year later, I heard the dungeon guard's rough voice at the door to solitary say, "Welcome to my department! This is a pleasure, Major, this is a pleasure. Come on inside and I'll show you the place. I was beginning to think, Major, you had forgotten all about solitary. I certainly welcome this chance to meet our new warden. Come on in!"

The guard and the stranger were now walking down the big solitary room, and as the two came into line with my vision, I instantly recognized the man whom the guard called Major. He was the new warden, and none other than my Alameda County man, the very one whom I had followed and watched so persistently during my wanderings from the straitjacket.

Overcome by emotion, I staggered back from the barred door. Now there could be no more doubt. My experiences in the straitjacket were real. I had never seen this man in the flesh prior to those strange events.

For a moment then, I forgot the new warden, and my mind flashed out to the town of fruit and flowers and the face of the little girl in the school room. I wondered if I would sometime meet her, too.

I heard my name. It was the Major asking the guard to show him my cell.

He entered and stood looking at me for a long time without saying a word, evidently lost in the horror of the gruesome object before him. His eyes were moist as he said, "Morrell, I am the new warden. Three weeks ago I took charge of San Quentin. From the very first day I have been busy investigating your case.

"You were accused of smuggling firearms in here, for the purpose of leading a mutiny. You were convicted on the evidence presented and sentenced to solitary confinement for the balance of your life. But my investigation of your case has proved that you were not guilty, but rather that you were the victim of a prison plot by a scoundrel who tried to profit by your misfortune.

"When the Board of Prison Commissioners held their meeting yesterday, I presented the facts and demanded that your sentence to solitary be revoked. Now I have come to release you. You have been most unjustly treated. I shall do all in my power to right that wrong while I am warden at San Quentin."

One day not long after I was released from solitary, the Captain of the Yard came over to me with the message that the Major wanted to see me immediately.

"I have sent for you for a special purpose," said the Major. "The position of Head Trusty is vacant for the fourth time in twenty-eight years. I know that you can fill the duties of Head Trusty, and all I ask is that you give me your word of honor as a man not to betray my trust in you."

We shook hands, we two who were so differently situated and apparently so far apart, thus cementing a friendship that was to last until death.

In strictest confidence he then told me how he had come to accept the wardenship of San Quentin. At first he refused it, having retired from active service. But the new governor of the state had asked him a second time, and while the two conversed over the phone, this man, sitting in his study, pencil in hand, unconsciously tapped upon a scratch pad. He finally promised the governor that he would think the matter over.

He hung up the receiver and, glancing at the paper, noticed that something had been written on it while he was talking. Seizing the pad, he read the name Ed. Morrell. He looked at it questioningly. It bothered him, and, unable to solve the enigma, he called up a friend who was a state official. Through him he learned that the name was that of the notorious "Dungeon Man of San Quentin."

The next day he told the governor that he had decided to accept his offer. "That's how I happen to be here," he said.

"I have never given much thought to the supernatural," he went on, "but I certainly would like to have you explain the riddle of how your name came to be written on that scratch pad!"

I smiled as I said, "Someday, Warden, about four years hence, I will make it all plain to you."

Four years later, as he had predicted, Ed. Morrell was given a pardon by Acting Governor Warren R. Porter, and left San Quentin a free man. And, also as predicted, the Governor delivered the pardon in person. Ed. Morrell devoted the rest of his life to campaigning for prison reform, and was instrumental in bringing to an end the legal use of the straitjacket and other instruments of torture in prisons.

But what about the young girl whom he had met in the "town of fruit and flowers"? The story ends with the solution to that puzzle.

The affair of the little girl troubled me. It was the one big link in my chain of experiences which I had not been able to piece together after my release from prison. I had made a trip to the little town and had gone to the school without asking directions of anyone. I located the desk near the window and from that point back-trailed to her home, only to find that the place was occupied by strangers. She had moved away and was now living somewhere in San Francisco.

But I was not discouraged. I knew I must wait for fate to untangle the threads that mysteriously drew me to her. And, like all good things in my life, it came about when least expected and at a moment when my thoughts were furthest from the quest.

Quite by chance I had met a friend in San Francisco. Before we parted I promised to call at a certain address for another meeting. It was nearly nine o'clock at night when I found time to keep the engagement.

I rang the bell and stood waiting. A young woman of about eighteen opened the door. From the bright hall light I could plainly see her face. I recognized her instantly. "Good God," I thought. "She is my little girl!"

My first impulse was to ask if she remembered me, but then common sense came to my rescue. Still, I could see that she gazed fixedly at me, just as she had years before when I stood near her desk. Yes, there was something in her memory and now, wonder of wonders, she was smiling.

In an effort to hide my confusion, I politely asked for the friend I had called to see. In the sweetest voice imaginable she told me my friend was out and was not expected until late; then she invited me to come in and wait.

I offered some apology and declined, but promised to call again. The door closed, and I walked down the street like one floating in air.

After our formal introduction, when she learned who I was, she confided to me that her most interesting study at the university was sociology, and that she had always had a dream that someday she would center her life work on the great problem of prison reform. Then she asked if I would help her in her studies.

From that time on we were almost inseparable, but it was a long while before I confided to her the secret of our strange association. I was overjoyed when she confessed that she believed it all. As a little girl, she had seen me in her daydreams.

We were sitting on the highest rock overlooking the ocean, near the Cliff House. Her hand was resting in mine. We had been talking about the coincidence of our meeting. She turned suddenly and, with the frank expression which had so impressed me in her childhood, looked straight into my eyes.

"I have known you always," she said. "The moment I opened that door, I recognized you as the man in stripes who had come to me in a vision in the school room. It is surprising, but I have felt your influence guiding me from that day to this."

I was happy beyond measure, but a thousand times happier still when she promised to be my wife after her school days had ended. Thus was completed the chain of my prophecies. The last, the best one of all.

Jack London's novel *The Jacket* (originally entitled *The Star Rover*) is a fictionalized version of Ed. Morrell's experiences.

THE BOY WHO WAS ONCE A MAN

by Elaine Hamilton

This is the story of a boy in India who claimed to remember a former life. While unusual even in Asia, this kind of claim does not create as much stir there as it would in the West. For millions of Hindus and Buddhists, rebirth, or reincarnation, is an accepted religious belief.

For the American psychiatrist Ian Stevenson, however, rebirth is a subject for scientific study. He has investigated dozens of alleged cases, most of which involved people in Asia or the Middle East. Not all, though. One of the most impressive cases is that of Edward W. Ryall, an Englishman who seems to possess total recall of a former life in seventeenth-century England. Ryall tells about it in his book *Born Twice*, to which Dr. Stevenson contributed the introduction.

Dr. Stevenson does not think these cases furnish unquestionable proof of reincarnation, so he merely calls them "suggestive" of it. However, the other theories that have been offered to explain these strange "far memories" seem to him to be no more convincing than reincarnation, and often less so.

The information that follows was published by Ian Stevenson in the *Journal of the American Society for Psychical Research*. Some facts have been omitted and others rearranged to make a less scientific but more interesting narrative. The Indian names have been changed slightly to make them easier for American readers.

Bishen Kapoor was born on February 7, 1921, in the city of Bareilly, India. When he was only ten months old, he began to babble something that sounded like "Pilvit" or "Pilivit." There is a town named Pilibhit about 50 kilometers from Bareilly, but the Kapoor family did not know anybody there.

When Bishen was one-and-a-half and could speak more plainly, he asked how far it was to Pilibhit and said he wanted to go there. He was, of course, refused; but once when he was about four his father took him and his brother to a family wedding in a town on the other side of Pilibhit. As soon as the train stopped at the Pilibhit station and the name was called, Bishen insisted that they should get off. "I used to live here," he said.

By now this was no news to his family, because since the age of three he had been regaling them with tales about his former life in Pilibhit. His parents had tried to keep the matter quiet, because there is a superstition that children who claim to remember earlier lives do not linger long in this one. However, they never punished or scolded him for talking about it. In fact, the tolerance they showed was remarkable, considering the unflattering terms in which he compared their poor home with the mansion he said he had had in Pilibhit.

He said that in the other life he had been Laxmi Narain, the son of a wealthy landowner. He had lived in a large, two-story house that had its own shrine room (or "chapel") and separate apartments for men and women. His father had been well-loved for his many generous gifts to charity, and at his death had received a sumptuous funeral attended by a huge throng of mourners.

After his father's death, Laxmi Narain spent much of his inheritance on luxury and good times. He was fond of wine, rohu fish, and parties at which beautiful girls entertained by singing and dancing. His neighbor Sunder Lal, who had a large house with a green gate, apparently had similar tastes. He often gave parties, complete with dancing girls, in his courtyard.

In his previous life, Bishen said, he had attended the Government School near the river, where he had gone through the sixth grade. He had known three languages: Hindi, Urdu, and English. (The Kapoor family spoke only Hindi.)

Up to the time he was seven, Bishen not only talked about the life of Laxmi, he also tried to revive its more attractive features. He would ask for money and would cry bitterly when his father, an ill-paid clerk in the railway service, told him he could not have it. When his mother dressed him in cotton clothes he would tear them off and demand silk ones. "I wouldn't give these clothes even to my servants!" he would say contemptuously.

The Kapoor family were members of a caste (social class) that considered it sinful to eat meat or fish or to drink alcohol. But this didn't stop Bishen from wanting all three, since as Laxmi Narain he had always had them. When he was refused meat at home, he found ways of getting an occasional meal at the homes of other people who served it. "Even my servant wouldn't eat the food cooked here," he told his long-suffering mother.

At one point the Kapoors had some brandy in the house for medicinal purposes. Suspicious because the bottle seemed to have less in it every time she checked, Bishen's older sister managed to catch him drinking it one day. She reproached him, but he only retorted, "I'm used to drinking!"

Although self-indulgent, Laxmi Narain had evidently been generous, too. One day Mr. Kapoor remarked that he was thinking of buying a watch, and Bishen overheard him. "Don't buy, Papa," he advised. "When I go to Pilibhit I'll get you three watches from a Moslem watch dealer whom I set up in business there." This claim was verified later when they did go to Pilibhit. The Moslem watch dealer had moved away, but people in the area who knew him said that Laxmi Narain had given him 500 rupees, a huge sum in those days, to start his business.

The trip to Pilibhit came about at the suggestion of K.K.N. Sahay, a lawyer who happened to hear about Bishen's memories. Sahay interviewed the boy, writing down his statements about his life as Laxmi Narain. Then he persuaded Mr. Kapoor that they should go to Pilibhit to see if the statements were true or not. Accordingly, on August 1, 1926, Mr. Sahay, Mr. Kapoor, Bishen, and Bishen's brother Bipan took the train to Pilibhit.

The first place they went to was the Government School, which Bishen said was not the one he had attended. He was right — the school was now in a different building.

Next they drove to the neighborhood of the Narain mansion. As they passed Sunder Lal's house, Bishen got down from the carriage and called attention to the gate. It was still green, although the paint was somewhat faded. Bishen also pointed out the courtyard where the parties had been held.

When they came to the empty Narain mansion, the boy shouted that this was his house. He went in and walked around as if he owned the place. But the building was in very poor condition, and this moved him to angry tears. "Nobody even cared enough to repair the house after my death!" he complained. One of the staircases had collapsed and been scattered amidst the debris on the lower floor; when asked where it had been, Bishen pointed to the correct spot. He also showed where the shrine room had been, and located the women's quarters on the upper floor, referring to them by the Urdu word *masurate* instead of the Hindi word *zenana*. Pointing to a door of the house, he said, "There was a kopal [lock] on this." *Kopal* is an Urdu word; the Kapoor family used the Hindi word for lock, *tala*.

An old photograph of Laxmi Narain and his father was brought by a relative of the family. "There is Har Narain," said Bishen, pointing to the man in the picture, "and here" — pointing to a boy sitting on a chair — "am I."

The last stop on the tour was the old Government School building. Bishen recognized it immediately and led the way up a staircase to the top of the building. There he pointed out the River Deuha flowing past the back of the old school. He was asked to identify the room where Class VI had met, and he did so. By this time a sizable crowd had gathered, and two of Laxmi's old classmates were in it. These two now stepped forward and said that Bishen was right. Then they asked him, "What was our teacher's name?" Bishen did not give the name but described the teacher, correctly, as a fat, bearded fellow.

The Superintendent of Police, who was also in the crowd, called out, "Now tell us about your wife and children."

"I had none," answered Bishen. "I was steeped in wine and women and never thought of marrying."

"What was the name of your favorite girl friend?" asked someone else. At first Bishen ignored the question, but after it had been repeated several times he reluctantly answered, "Padma."

At home Bishen had never been loath to discuss his girl friend, although he had apparently never mentioned her name before this. Nor had he ever hesitated to tell — even to boast — about the act that had brought a violent end to their relationship. But on this occasion in Pilibhit, perhaps the boy Bishen was trying to avoid questions about what the man Laxmi had done.

Laxmi Narain was walking by Padma's house one day when he saw another man, a rival for her love, come out of the door. Without warning, Laxmi seized his gun from his servant, who was carrying it, and shot the man dead.

Afterwards he hid in the garden of his house, living on food that his mother smuggled to him. Court records show that he was eventually involved in a trial connected with this murder, but he was never convicted. Apparently, however, he thought it wise to move to another town, Shahjehanpur, where he got a job working for the Oudh railway. He died there of fever and lung trouble on December 15, 1918, at the age of 32.

Sometime after Bishen's trip to Pilibhit, the mother of Laxmi Narain came to visit him. Not only did the boy recognize her, but he also called her by the name that Laxmi would have used. He called her "Bahu," whereas he called his own mother "Amma."

Mrs. Narain was impressed, but she nevertheless administered a little test to Bishen. "Did you fly kites?" she asked him first.

"Yes."

"With whom did you compete in kite flying?" (Indian children make a sport of trying to knock each other's kites out of the air by entangling or cutting the opponent's kite string.)

Bishen answered: "I competed with every kite that came within range of mine, but in particular I competed with Sunder Lal."

"Did you throw away my pickles?"

"Yes, I did, but how could you expect me to eat worms?"

(Mrs. Narain was referring to one time when her canned pickles got rotten and there were worms in the jars. She took the worms out, but kept the pickles in the sun. Much to her annoyance, Laxmi threw the pickles away.)

"Did you ever enter into the civil service?"

"Yes, I worked for some time for the Oudh railway."

"Who was your servant?"

"My servant was Maikua, a dark, short Kahar. [The Kahar caste is quite low in the social scale.] He was my favorite cook."

On a later occasion, Bishen was questioned by other people who had known Laxmi Narain.

Q: "Didn't you use to sleep on a bamboo charpoy with no bedding?" (A charpoy is a rude cot used mostly by poor people.)

A: "You obviously never saw my bed. I had a good one with an ornamental headboard, and I had a thick cover on it. I also had two pillows at the head and two at the foot."

Q: (by a former teacher): "What did I teach at Pilibhit?"

A: "You taught Hindi."

Not only were Bishen's answers correct, but in one particular case they were even worth money to the Narain family. It was thought that before his death, Mr. Narain had hidden some treasure, telling no one but his son Laxmi where it was. Since Laxmi's own death had come unexpectedly, he had apparently never seen fit to pass on the secret. The Narains had searched for the treasure without success — and they really needed it, for between Mr. Narain's charities and Laxmi's fondness for high living, the family fortune had been exhausted. So Mrs. Narain asked Bishen where the treasure was, and he obligingly led the way to a room in the house in Pilibhit. They searched that room and found the treasure.

Bishen also received a visit from Laxmi's sweetheart, Padma, who came to his house with her younger sister, Ganga, when the boy was about six. Bishen recognized Padma, but it was the younger sister whose lap he sat on. Ganga was some six years younger than Padma, so she was about the age that Padma had been at the time of Laxmi's death. "You are a small child," Padma said to him ruefully. "I have grown old."

She was exaggerating: she was probably in her early thirties at the time. However, at their next meeting she had indeed reached late middle age.

That meeting took place in 1944, when Bishen Kapoor was 23 years old. He was working in a tax-collecting office in a town 80 kilometers north of Pilibhit. One day three or four women came into the office, and one of them attracted Bishen's attention. "Aren't you Padma?" he asked her. She answered, "Yes." Overcome with emotion, Bishen embraced her — and then collapsed in a faint.

That evening he bought a bottle of wine (something he had not indulged in for many years) and went to Padma's house in hopes of renewing their old friendship. But Padma was not glad to see him. "I'm old enough to be your mother," she said. "Please go away. You lost everything in your previous life, and now you want to lose everything again." And with that she picked up the bottle of wine and smashed it. The two never saw each other again.

Bishen Kapoor related this incident to Dr. Ian Stevenson in 1969. At that time he was 48 years old and had been faithfully married to a woman of his own caste for 26 years. Like his parents, his wife was a vegetarian, so he sometimes took meals in restaurants where he could get meat and fish. He had long since lost his taste for alcohol, however, and he said he was content with the modest home and plain clothing which were all he could afford on his tax-collector's salary. His only regret, he told Dr. Stevenson, was that his present life offered no scope for the generous impulses he had carried over from the last, when, as Laxmi Narain, he had not only spent money freely but had also given much away.

He explained that his memories of the former life had begun to fade when he was about seven, and that now there was only one event that he still recalled vividly. That event was the murder of his rival in a fit of drunken jealousy. As a child, he had boasted about this murder, but as a man he remembered it with remorse. In fact, he now believed that it was probably this act, more than any other, that had caused him to be "demoted" from wealth in his former life to poverty in this one.

But he also told Dr. Stevenson that his hopes for the next life, if he should have one, did not center on riches. Rather, he said, he would like to be born with superior intelligence and, perhaps, to gain fame by some important achievement.